Endorsements for Jungle Prophet: Into the Fire

In the tradition of C.S. Lewis, Sharon Swan presents the readers of her novels with biblical truths wrapped in engaging stories. I am happy to commend her latest work, *Jungle Prophet: Into the Fire*.
—**Robert L. Plummer, Ph.D.,** Chairman, New Testament Department, *Southern Baptist Theological Seminary*

***

In the book *Jungle Prophet: Into the Fire*, jungle animals take on human characteristics. Love, hate, jealousy, forgiveness, deception, self-reliance, and self-sacrifice are shown as the animals try to find their way through grim times. Filled with action and romance, the book captivates readers of both sexes. Written for the young teen, the symbolism showing God's love shines through. The accurate descriptions of the animals and topography of the Amazon Jungle are refreshing. The questions at the end of each chapter lead the reader to self-reflection and make the book an excellent discussion guide for teen leaders.
—**Mr. Joe Warner,** Retired Middle School Social Studies Teacher

***

The sequel to Sharon Swan's *Jungle Prophet* is as fast-paced, vivid, and gripping as the original. *Jungle Prophet: Into the Fire* recasts the battle of good and evil, set in the Amazon jungle, and follows the new Prophet Rhett, who is humble, chosen, and prone to self-doubt (thus reminiscent of Moses) as he tries to rule and protect a diverse, endangered animal kingdom, in accordance with divine law. Fast-paced, meaningful action and engaging characters will capture a preteen's imagination. The clarity of description, fresh and vivid metaphors, and clear, crisp prose are coupled with a bonus: Swan ends each chapter with thought-provoking questions to lead young readers to more deeply and personally enter the story and its meaning. I definitely recommend.

—**Kelly Wilkinson, Ph.D.,** Retired Lawyer: Law Degree with honors from LSU, MFA from *University of the South*

***

I enjoyed the allegorical aspects of the world created in *Jungle Prophet: Into the Fire*. The theme was easy to understand, and the story included interesting animal characters. The fast-moving plot made me want to find out what happened next; I read it in two days.

—**John Young**, 13-year-old fan

Jungle Prophet
Into the Fire

Sharon R. Swan

Published by KHARIS PUBLISHING, an imprint of
KHARIS MEDIA LLC.
Copyright © 2025 Sharon R. Swan
ISBN-13: 978-1-63746-283-6
ISBN-10: 1-63746-283-2
Library of Congress Control Number: 2024950132

All KHARIS PUBLISHING products are available at special quantity
discounts for bulk purchase for sales promotions, premiums, fund-raising,
and educational needs. For details, contact:

Kharis Media LLC
Tel: 1-630-909-3405
support@kharispublishing.com
www.kharispublishing.com

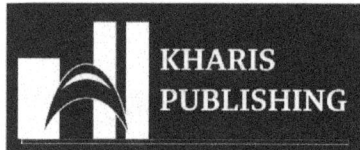

To the author of all good stories and maker of dreams - my deepest thanks.
To Marty who has always believed in me more than I believe in myself.
To Lillian, Anna, Sarah, and Isaac - I am so proud of who you're becoming.
To Mom and Dad - thanks for providing a strong Christian foundation.
To TBC youth group - thanks for being the best group of kids ever.

Contents

Chapter

01

The Dream

"**G**o, Mara! Go, now!"

I scream the words, but why? And why does my throat feel like it's stuffed with a thousand dandelions?

Sweat trickles into my eyes, blurring my vision. Why am I so hot—scorching hot?

Where's Mara? Gray smoke—it's everywhere—it's suffocating. Why did I push her away from me; where did she go? Confusion and despair wrestle in my mind like angry winds in a storm.

The smoke fills my nostrils, my eyes, my lungs—fear fills my heart. I'm not safe. I need to follow Mara, but how can I follow when I don't know where she went?

I look around. Lightning streaks the sky. Fire, there's fire in the jungle. Panic rises like bile from my stomach. I need to warn the animals. They need to get to safety. Then I know it, I feel it. The Wimba. The Wimba will be safe.

I'm falling now, looking desperately for a branch. There must be one somewhere, but all I see is black and orange swirling ash.

I yell for help, but the wind rushing by sucks and scrambles my call. My tail: it burns. My tail is burning. "Aaaaah."

✷✷✷

The Prophet jerked awake on one of the higher branches of the Wimba tree. In sleep, his tail had twisted around the supporting limb like a snake coiled along a willow vine. Rhett bent over and coaxed his tail muscles into releasing their grip, noticing as he did, several patches of missing fur. The limb, now covered with brown kinkajou fur, looked like an over-sized caterpillar.

"The same dream." He moaned. "Three times now, and it's getting worse." He gazed around his tree home in the middle of Sanchia's Sanctuary, trying to reassure himself that it was in fact a dream. *I wish Saloma were here; maybe she could tell me what the dream means – if it even means anything.*

His tail still drooped when thoughts of his beloved mentor and friend came to mind. She'd been gone two moons, and still many times Rhett would think of things to ask her, only to then remember her passing. The wizened sloth and former Prophet had died so suddenly, sacrificing herself to the claws of Tirgato to save Rhett's best friend, Giran.

The evil jaguar, Tirgato, was executed by his eldest son, Adan. Of course, Tirgato had it coming to him—he killed Saloma. His was a just death for the ancient crime of striking down a Prophet. Tirgato's absence brought relief to the jungle region of Sanchia, but Giran's leaving weighed heavy like one of the giant boulders lining the Great River.

Giran was Tirgato's youngest son who had left Sanchia willingly to try to find more cats in neighboring regions. More predators were needed to replace the jaguars his father had banished in his evil

10

rampage against all who challenged his self-assumed authority. Giran hadn't been gone long, but nothing seemed right in Sanchia without his best friend.

Rhett sighed, but with his next deep breath, the smell of smoke tickled his nostrils. Eyes watering, he craned his neck in all directions, searching for the flames. But for now, only the smell of smoke, not even its dark appearance, hung heavy in the air. *Dream. Reality. Which is it?* But with the nightmare's increasing vividness, came a foreboding of troubles thicker than the lingering smell of smoke.

The crackling of flames interrupted his pondering. His heart flipped over as it resumed the panicked pace from his dream. The fire—is it real? Is it near?

"Prophet?" called Elder Horado a little louder from the base of the tree, demanding attention from Sanchia's leader. The old marsh deer was directly underneath the Wimba now, prancing around the trunk.

Rhett craned his neck in all directions, but not seeing anything out of the ordinary, he abandoned his search for flames. Directing his attention instead to the elder, the mystery source of his "fire" came to light. The crackling was Elder Horado's hooves crushing the blades of sparse, dry grass.

Rhett rolled his eyes at his overactive imagination as he started down the Wimba. Was his imagination playing tricks on his mind? Or was it the strange dream that had a way of crossing the boundaries into reality?

"When's this dry spell going to end?" Rhett asked the elder, filling the air with trite conversation as he climbed gingerly down, favoring his still raw tail. Rhett knew the elder had no more idea how to read the weather than he did, but it did serve to stop the deer from pawing at every patch of grass at the foot of the Wimba. He didn't expect a response and didn't get one – not that that deterred him from continuing the one-sided conversation. "It's never gone this long without rain."

The unpleasant thought slowed his descent as he paused to search the sky for any sign of a cloud. The uniquely long dry spell that had settled over Sanchia did nothing to aid the starving gatherers of Sanchia. They were already suffering from overly crowded jungle conditions caused by the lack of cat predators. Drought on top of predator/prey imbalance made for a jungle crammed with cantankerous creatures.

When Rhett had finished climbing most of the way down, he stopped to perch on the lowest branch that ran almost parallel to the ground.

"Now, Elder. What can I help you with?"

The elder stepped back several paces to avoid craning his large neck, pawing nervously at the packed dirt before speaking. "She delivered—about high noon. I don't know if she thought our day animals wouldn't notice or wouldn't care, but one of my grandsires spotted her along one of the northern spider branches of Pooto creek."

"Are you sure it was her?"

"I'm sure. I went and saw for myself but didn't approach her. No animal in his right mind would go near her now. She'd eat an animal twice my size and look around for more."

Rhett jumped to the ground and paced back and forth in front of the elder. "She's never delivered in Sanchia? Why now, even after we warned her? Why does she insist on being difficult?"

"Saloma's been here in the past, and now... Fattima's testing the waters, seeing how far she can push a new Prophet."

"But doesn't she know it means death to her offspring? What mother would do that?"

"Only if you follow through with your threat, and even then, she doesn't care about her babies. She's had numerous birthings. Frankly, I'm surprised any survive at all. I heard from a cousin in Placero that she ate over half her brood last delivery when she had trouble finding prey."

Rhett stared at the elder with mouth open. "Half her offspring?"

"Don't be so surprised. This is a snake, and not only a snake, an anaconda. They have no conscience, no sense of right and wrong. They don't even have a respect for the Sovereign Himself."

Rhett shook his head, still in disbelief. "If she did want to deliver here, all she had to do was come and swear allegiance to the Sovereign."

"You mean the Sovereign she doesn't recognize," the elder said with a smirk.

Rhett huffed. "She would have had free access to use Sanchia as her nursery. Truth be told, it might have been a good thing seeing that each of her young ones would grow to be a predator."

Elder Horado snorted his approval. "I agree, Prophet, though many Sanchians still question your call for more predators."

Both were silent as they contemplated the worsening food shortage. Rhett's mind again wandered to Giran and his mission to bring home cats.

The whooshing sound of the Wimba birds landing above stirred both from their thoughts. Azul, the chief messenger, perched on the branch recently abandoned by Rhett.

"Prophet, prophet. Many small snakes thrive; many snakes writhe. What to do? What to do?"

Rhett sighed. This wasn't a command he wanted to give. Personally, he wished the law wasn't so clear on the issue, but it was. For a reason unknown to even Saloma—a reason rooted from a transgression that occurred countless seasons ago—a snake must swear allegiance before giving birth in a region. Usually, this was not a problem as Rhett had already issued allowances for many snake mamas, but Fattima was intent on stirring the waters. Now, the law declared that her offspring had to be eliminated.

"But," he reasoned, "a few more predators wouldn't hurt, especially until Giran gets back." Rhett closed his eyes and shook his head in an attempt torid himself of the temptation to ignore the law.

"Azul, summon Elder Brayan. Please tell them to come to the Wimba right away with every young male in his clan. Wait, not here, that will take too much time. Tell them to meet me at the Northern Fork. Also, inform Elder Mochuelo that we need him and a few of his best hunters tonight. The owls can hunt from the air, the otters from the water."

A blue rush of feathers lit from the Wimba. Rhett would need to swing fast to not keep the otters waiting, and he already knew the owls would beat him there.

Elder Horado cleared his throat. "This won't be popular, Rhett. A snake hunt hasn't been done since, well, I've never seen one. Heard about 'em, and from what I've heard, they can be brutal."

Rhett wrung his paws and looked pleadingly at the elder. "What can I do, Horado? We warned her, threatened her even. She knows exactly what the Law says. She's put me between tooth and claw. If I don't act now—I disobey the Sovereign. Plus, Fattima and the rest of the jungle will know my threats are nothing. But if I do issue the snake hunt, I risk looking like a mad kinkajou, killing babies for the fun of it and not caring a whit about the predator balance of Sanchia."

After a moment's pause, the two looked at each other square on. The ancient elder's brown eyes glistened with the soft sheen of sympathy. "You're right. Neither option seems altogether right. But if you have to choose, choose the Sovereign and His law. That's what Saloma would have done."

Rhett quickly averted his eyes to avoid the elder detecting his annoyance. He knew the old deer didn't mean to constantly bring up Saloma. But would he always live in her shadow? Probably, but would it always irritate?

Rhett pushed those unflattering thoughts aside. "I agree, Elder. This is the path we must follow. But I do fear the consequences. Fattima will not be happy about her brood. Even if she cares nothing for them, she's going to care that she didn't get away with having them here. And the rest of the animals …."

"You can't worry about what every animal thinks. Do what's best."

14

Rhett shook his head in agreement, but he couldn't dismiss the nagging thought that this decision would come back to bite him."

Discussion Questions:

1. Is there someone in your life that you look to for guidance? If so, praise God for that person and consider how you can thank them for being a blessing.

2. If you have to make a big decision, what resources has God provided to help you make good choices?

Chapter

02

On a Quest

It had been two days since water. Giran had to change course—move out of the wastelands long enough to at least hydrate. The scent of a creek drifted by in the wind, revealing itself to be about an hour northeast. This wasn't the best location to deviate from his plan. He was nearing the southern boundaries of Altura, the region where Adan's clan had supposedly settled. Vanción, the region north of Altura, was his destination, his hope of a territory filled with hospitable jaguars, but he needed to get past Adan's homeland first.

It hadn't been long since Adan and him had met up in Sanchia. Before then, he had never known about his older half-brother. Adan had tried to get him to conspire against and murder his evil father, Tirgato, but Giran couldn't get himself to do it. Adan had felt betrayed and made it clear that if they ever crossed paths again, there would be trouble.

Giran didn't care for any impromptu family reunions, but there wasn't a choice unless he wanted to die of thirst in the wasteland. He had hoped to take refuge along his journey on the western edges of Placero, but as of yet, the jaguar hadn't noticed an opening in the high cliffs that formed the border. A valley that separated the highlands of Placero and Altura. He'd have to stop there. With any luck, the creek would be easy to find and access, and he could veer back into the wastelands without much loss in time.

It wasn't long before Giran turned his head right and crept into a mist-drenched valley hemmed between towering mountain peaks. In the distance, the tops of Altura's green cliffs lost their definition, blending effortlessly into the evening sky. He heard the trickle of the spring that wound its way through the small risings of the valley. The stream surely marked the border between regions. Staring at the cliffs of Altura in the distance made him shiver with the remembrance of Adan's threats. The two brothers were to never cross paths again. Giran would need to make quick work of this pit stop and be back in the wastelands no later than sunrise.

An urgency—deeper than the desire to avoid his brother—welled up inside, prompting him to rush. Rhett was counting on him, and no one had ever trusted him before, especially with such an important task. He must be successful and find cats that would migrate back with him to Sanchia. Only then would his region be able to recover from the starvation that was plaguing the gatherers.

It would seem as if this would be an easy task, but Giran instinctively knew better. Cats were notoriously stubborn and headstrong creatures. Once comfortable, they were close to impossible to budge. He had to find cats open to change. And not just males, either. No, Sanchia would need both males and females to thrive.

Giran warily approached the creek, eyes darting to make sure nothing escaped his attention. He was drier than week-old scat, but caution won over desire. Dipping his paw twice, he carefully searched for snake vibrations. He had learned that lesson the hard way, and this time, no prophet was around to save him.

When he was satisfied that no predators lurked in the area, his muscles relaxed. He lowered his head to the surface of the brown water and drank until his tongue tired from lapping.

Now that his thirst was satisfied, he was more aware of the gnawing in his stomach. A short break to find food wouldn't cost him much time. It might actually save him time in the long run. With a good meal in his belly, he could reach the northern region without another stop.

Giran perked his dominant ear to the sky, listening intently for prey. He could stay in this position for as long as needed, but in this case, detection was instant. Heavy hooves pounded nearby, bruising the earth under their hefty weight. A wonderful odor drifted by on the eastern wind—cattle. Beef hadn't been available for seasons, not since a stray herd had wandered past Sanchia. He and his father had eaten their fill for several days before the herd moved on.

With light and eager steps, Giran followed his nose across the stream and into the valley cradled at the base of Altura's highlands. Patches of brown littered the green field but overall, the land fared better here under the extended drought than Sanchia. That's probably why the cattle had gathered here: plenty of water and better pasture.

He quickened his step, and over the next small rise and turn, a good-sized number of cattle came into view. Giran took a moment to look over the fattened herd. Assessing the animals before the hunt saved him time and energy. It also was the Sovereign's way of ensuring that the older or weaker animals were hunted. But after looking the herd over, he shook his head. None appeared sick. After a moment of deliberation, he chose one that appeared to be long in the tooth.

Blending with the moving shadows drifting across the valley, Giran patiently and noiselessly crept alongside the grazing herd. When the targeted cow was in a perfect position, about twenty tail lengths, he leapt toward his prey with a burst of energy.

Three strides in and he was ready to pounce. Every muscle was tight—his eyes focused on the target. Then a crack rendered the air, a crack foreign to Giran. His back leg collapsed, dragging the rest of him down. Dirt mushroomed as he skidded to a halt.

The herd was at first frozen in horror at the sound—for just a second. Then they came alive and charged in madness across the field. Unfortunately for Giran, he was in their direct path. He pulled himself up by his forelegs, intent on jumping away from the coming stampede. But his back leg didn't respond. *Why is it burning? Why can't I run?*

The cows closed in on him. He tried to dodge their hooves and their massive bodies as they tussled and shoved while charging along. It was too much—the cows too numerous and frantic. The last thing Giran felt was a massive kick to the head before darkness overtook him.

Discussion Questions

1. Have you ever had someone counting on you for something? How did that make you feel?

2. It's exciting to be trusted with a task. Right before Jesus left to go back to Heaven, He said in Matthew 28:19, "Therefore go and make disciples of all nations, baptizing them in the name of the Father and of the Son and of the Holy Spirit, and teaching them to obey everything I have commanded you." (NIV) What are some ways that you can help make disciples?

Chapter

03

Snake Hunt

Rhett could hear Elder Brayan well before he reached the Northern Fork. Of all the animals in Sanchia, the barking otters were the loudest. The squealing monkeys carousing in the nearby mango grove had nothing on the otter clan.

The night animals stirred, adding to the symphony as the shadows on the jungle floor darkened. *It's good timing, at least for snaring snake. The empty bellies of the waking otters will add incentive to their mission, and owls are always ready to hunt—hungry or not. If need be, I'll call in the larger birds even though they hesitate to hunt in the understory. No creature, even the brief life of the baby anacondas, should be wasted.*

Rhett swung out on a large rock out-cropping that split the waters of Flujo de Vida flowing south from the highlands. Moss-covered and slimy, Rhett had to plant all four of his paws with care. He tip-pawed to the edge and sighed as he looked down where brown eddies swirled lazily around the darkened base of the rock. Barely a trickle flowed compared to seasons past. This keystone rock was normally bombarded by rushing waves, but the dry season had lingered too long. Even the Flujo de Vida was slowing.

Rhett felt rather than heard the rush of wind ruffle his fur as Elder Mochuelo landed deftly on the rock beside him.

"Good evening, Prophet." The elder owl bowed his head and spoke in a voice deeper than a full-grown caiman. "The owls are near—through the branches they peer—anxiously awaiting their dinner."

Rhett cocked his head and studied Elder Mochuelo from squinted eyes. He hadn't spent much time with the standoffish owls. But now, he wished he had made more of an effort to understand the creatures. Were they followers, foes, or something in between? He shrugged. *Today, at least, they're on my side*. When all was even again in Sanchia, he'd make it a priority to understand them better.

The gray feathered owl must have known by Rhett's open-mouthed stare that he was the object of the Prophet's musings. However, he gave no response whether it bothered him or if he relished the look of confusion on the young kinkajou's face.

Elder Brayan, head of the otter clan, had seen the owl land and crawled up the side of the rock to join the two, his claws making deep gashes along the green moss. The meaty elder, who was at least a tail length long, sported stripes along both sides of his neck. These markings from a long-ago battle glowed a creamy orange under the last rays of the setting sun.

With both elders settled beside him, they all surveyed the scene below. None of the owls besides Elder Mochuelo were seen or heard, but that was to be expected. In the water surrounding the rock, at least fifteen chocolate brown hides dotted the surface—enough for the job. Elder Brayan barked a call to order, and the creek's volume quieted save a few periodic hums from the overly anxious youth.

Rhett wiped his clammy paws on his side fur, wishing he was back in the Wimba tree and not in front of a crowd about to institute the first snake hunt in seasons—maybe first ever in Sanchia. When the otters fidgeted in the water below, he took a deep breath and began.

21

"Proud otter clan, distinguished owls, I thank you for your ongoing loyalty to Sanchia and your service this evening. We recognize this situation is not one in which we rejoice. However, feelings must be set aside as we strive to obey the Sovereign and restore a just jungle society under His law. I know that each of you will be respectful as you carry out this task."

Rhett paused to glance at the elder at his side. The otter's glazed eyes were locked on something up creek. *Is he in deep thought about the hunt or just plain dreaming?* Rhett sighed. He was probably being long-winded again. Abandoning the rest of his planned speech, he skipped to the needed details.

"There are approximately sixty young anacondas. Please beware of Fattima. Know her position at all times. Keep a safe distance. Elder Mochuelo will rally the owls from the air; Elder Brayan will organize and lead the hunt from the water."

The aged otter stirred at the hearing of his name and called for the members of his clan individually, separating them into groups of three or four. In a matter of minutes, the otters were swimming in teams down the Flujo de Vida. The river would soon branch into numerous creeks, one of which was Potoo Creek, the site of the birthing. Elder Mochuelo had flown off unnoticed after Rhett's speech, leaving the Prophet alone on the rock.

The calls of the evening caracaras merged with the barks of the otters. If Rhett listened closely, he could just hear the writhing of snakes on the shallow mud bank. Maybe that was a bit much, maybe his conscience was getting to him. *Is this the right thing to do? Why did it have to come to this? Why didn't she listen?* Rhett's heart twisted as he mourned the small creatures he had sentenced to death, even if they were anacondas. He placed his face in both paws and rocked back and forth as his tears plopped like jungle rain into the muddy water.

When the calls of the otters quieted, Rhett knew it was over. Silence hung in the air like a ripened mango swinging on the breeze. Even though the owls had not been seen or heard, Rhett didn't doubt their effectiveness in the hunt. The owls were always successful on the hunt, frighteningly so if he thought about it.

He reached for a branch and swung from limb to limb across the muddy waters of the creek. On each side, the otters were feasting. They had called their families to join the meal, and the banks were strewn with chocolate brown hides. Eating their fill, these creatures at least would benefit from Fattima's rebellious choice.

Elder Brayan gave a sharp bark that grabbed Rhett's attention and halted his flight across the creek. Dangling on a vine, he turned back and located the elder eating with his family on the eastern side. He made his way over to the elder and sat beside him on the muddy bank. The old otter didn't speak—would have been rather impolite with a full mouth—but instead motioned with his head to take note farther downstream.

Fattima's long body bridged the creek on a sagging limb that dipped within a paw's length from the gentle ripples. She stared at him with bulging black eyes that looked like ominous full moons. He couldn't pry his attention away. A sudden chill permeated down his spine and straightened his tail. Elder Brayan waddled a short distance into the water—away from the others—and slapped his massive tail on the flat surface. Fattima didn't budge from her perch, but it was enough to break the death stare. Rhett nodded his thanks to the otter and turned to go.

"Prophet?" Elder Brayan called. "Prophet, I wouldn't come near these waters for a while – not till Fattima moves on. Stares like that mean one thing. Prophet or not, she's planning on killing you."

Another shudder went through his spine. He knew the elder's words summed up the situation correctly, but no one likes to hear that someone wants to eat you for breakfast. Normally, Rhett never felt fear, for his own life anyway. The law forbade the harming of a Prophet with the penalty of death. In Tirgato's case, the prophecy had come true by way of blindness after he clawed Saloma. In a jungle, blindness, and death were synonymous. Regardless of the prophecy and the measure of comfort it usually brought, Rhett felt the truth of Brayan's words. Murder lurked behind Fattima's stare.

Rhett stuck out his chest and tried to exude a confidence he didn't feel, but his planned flippant response got stuck somewhere between his brain and quivering chin. Rhett nodded—at least he could do that. He was turning away again when Elder Brayan called him back a second time.

"Prophet, would you do it again?"

Rhett stared into the eyes of the aged otter. They were every bit as dark in color as Fattima's had been. But instead of the darkness of a pit, it was the darkness of a restful and still evening. They were inviting like a cozy nook during a downpour. Rhett relaxed, wondering if Elder Brayan ever worried about anything. He finally shook his head and told himself to focus. "Do what again?"

"The snake hunt—would you do it again?"

Rhett couldn't answer that question—not now—not honestly. But he also didn't want to seem unsure of himself. He broke his stare with the elder before the otter could see the lurking fear and indecision and nodded the answer he assumed was expected. Grabbing the nearest vine, he swung off into the canopy, not waiting around for any other callbacks.

As Rhett made his way back to the Wimba, he prayed hard. Prayed for rain, prayed for Giran, prayed for Sanchia. Prayed and prayed and prayed. But he couldn't help wondering, was the Sovereign listening?

Discussion Questions

1. What would you say to Rhett if he confided to you that he wondered if the Sovereign actually heard his prayers?

2. Read Psalm 145:18-19. If you are a child of God, you never have to worry if your heavenly Father hears your prayers.

Chapter

04

Corazón

A voice called from the darkness—soft and tender. "It's okay, you're okay. Don't try to move."

Giran tried to force open his eyes. They were crusted shut. *Who's licking my ear? No one's licked my ear in seasons.*

Even though the grooming was heavenly, curiosity won over comfort, and Giran struggled to rouse himself. He tried to sit up, but a sharp pain from his right leg took his breath away. He abandoned the effort.

"My name is Cora, well Corazón, but everyone calls me Cora. I've been taking care of you."

Giran tensed at the sound of a feminine voice. He had never seen a female jaguar—not since his mom anyway—and that had been seasons ago.

He moaned, and this time it had nothing to do with the pain. *Great! My opportunity finally comes, and I can't even open my eyes.*

When Cora spoke again, he didn't feel her breath across his cheek. The disappointment in her distance was worse than the pain in his leg.

"Be still. I need to clean the wound on your leg."

Cora licked his angry leg. Even though it hurt when her rough tongue scraped across his thigh, the sensation of another jaguar—a feminine one at that—caring for him made him feel warmer than sunbathing at noon.

After what seemed to Giran as just a tail flick of glorious attention, she stopped. He sighed when he felt the softness of her body as she lay down next to him. Her scent—smell of fresh grass—was his last impression before drifting to sleep.

When he awoke, he was alone and cold. His eyes were still crusted shut, but this time he could move enough to lick his paw and groom his face. A thin mat of reeds—green and freshly gathered—separated him from a stone floor. Stone floor, stone walls, stone ceiling. Everything was solid except for an opening behind his head. The room was a cave, but a small one, more like a divot in a rock face.

Giran twisted around, trying to see out the entrance, but the pain in his leg hindered movement. After two more attempts, he sighed and laid his head back on the reed mat. He stared at the stone wall in front of him and watched as a deep shadow line rose from the floor and chased away the blush of sunlight.

"So, you're awake." The sound from the entrance encouraged him to move again, to twist toward her voice. She must have recognized his pain-filled attempt and walked into view.

Around her head glowed a soft orange halo from the last rays of sunlight. Her jaw was narrow, and when she opened her mouth to speak, her teeth shone white and smooth.

"You're up, but are you going to speak?" She smiled, studying him through gold-tinted eyes that were slanted in the most appealing way.

Giran, painfully aware of his awkward silence, tried to form words, but all he could get out of his parched lips was a moan.

"Wait here. I'll bring you some water. I should have brought it with me. Well of course you'll wait here. You can't very well move with that leg." She giggled and skittered away. Giran's urge to follow was as big as a Kapok, making his paws twitch in eagerness.

He was still sniffing her scent with some satisfaction when she returned with a coconut shell dangling from her mouth.

Ugg, please not coconut.

"Here, have some water." She said, carefully placing the shell beside him. "I tried my best not to spill any, but I can go back if you want more."

Giran tried to express his thanks, especially since it was water and not coconut milk, but words still wouldn't pass through his dry mouth. He gave up and slurped her offering. She had to go back to the creek and refill twice before Giran had his fill.

"Thanks, Cora." His voice sounded strange—even to him— scratchy strange like a newborn rat's call. "Cora's your name, right? You told me that last time I was awake. At least, I think you did."

"Yeah, it's Cora. What's your name?"

Giran drew a panicked blank as he stared into her eyes. The golden pools seemed to suck all rational thought from his mind. All he could think about was her scent and the sound of her panting. After a period of awkwardness, Giran blurted, "I'm not from around here."

Cora laughed, and it sounded like water skipping along the rocks.

"I kinda knew you weren't from around here. We, my family and I, know all the cats in Altura. But where are you from?"

Giran gasped. *Altura is Adan's home. What have I done? I'll be dead by daylight.*

His voice cracked. "Altura, are you sure?"

Cora rolled her eyes and cocked her head. "Pretty sure."

He huffed in frustration. *How? I was avoiding Altura, staying west in the badlands.* And then the last evening came to mind–his thirst, his detour into the border valley, a stampede.

He looked at Cora, who stared at him with a quizzical look. "Cora, how did I get here? The last thing I remember was a searing pain in my leg and then dodging cows."

"One of my father's scouts heard the stampede and investigated. He spotted you after the cattle had cleared and went to see if you were still alive."

"But how did they get me back here?"

"It took several of our strongest warriors to pull you into the caves. We have a large cattle hide for such things when needed."

Giran nodded and looked down at his hurt leg. Cora's eyes followed his as she stooped over to inspect the injury. He hesitated to ask more questions, to talk in general. Maybe Adan wouldn't find out he was here if he didn't have to give up any more info about himself. But what had happened? Maybe just a few more questions wouldn't hurt anything. "I heard a big crack right before my leg collapsed. Do you know what that was? Is it what caused my wound?"

"Haven't you ever heard one before? It was one of man's sticks—his lightning sticks. He points it at animals, and the next thing you know, they're hurt or even dead."

Giran stared back at her with wide eyes. "I've never been around humans much. I mean, they pass by my region on the Great River sometimes, but they don't hang around."

"Where did you say you were from again?"

Giran grinned. "I didn't say."

His response earned another one of those delightful laughs. *They're worth working for. I'm going to have to think of clever things to say more often.*

"We'll continue this discussion when you're in a more forthcoming mood."

She smiled and moved to the door. "Stay still; I'll bring you food when I come again. Your injury will take a few days to heal. The more cooperative you are now, the quicker you can get back to your mystery region."

Giran spent the rest of the long night alone, thinking and sleeping. He was thankful he hadn't answered Cora's personal questions. If Adan heard his name or even his region, he would have more injuries than a hurt leg. He needed to heal—quietly—and then somehow slip out of Altura unnoticed by his half-brother.

Maybe Cora will help? Then another thought raised his eyebrows and sent his tail swaying. *What if Cora comes with me?* It was just a nice idea—a dream. But for a dream, it was the best one he'd had in a long time.

Discussion Questions

1. Is withholding truth considered wise in some situations or is it a form of lying?

2. What are your favorite dreams?

Chapter

05

The Shipment

Rhett swung from branch to branch over Lower Belo Creek, periodically dipping his tail low enough to draw a path of curved ripples in the current. The sun shone straight above, so bright that Rhett had to squint in his search for the best swinging holds. He would have preferred the shipment to arrive in darkness, but he would prefer many things these days such as not having to deal with a drought on top of the food shortage caused by predator/prey imbalance. The purchase arriving today from Cantiga, a region northeast of Sanchia, was the largest food import ever recorded.

Would Saloma be disappointed in me, or would she approve? The thought persisted as he neared the mouth of the creek where it branched off from the Flujo de Vida. *How would she handle Sanchia's current crisis?*

Rhett bit his lip. He didn't know for sure. The food was extremely costly given the fact the highlands were also experiencing some measure of the drought, though he had heard it wasn't as severe. All the honey they had gathered still wasn't enough. He had to promise five tree yields of mango on next year's crop, assuming they had one.

Rhett rested on a lookout branch just south of the branch split. Azul, his ever-hovering messenger bird, had brought him word that the shipment was nearing Sanchia's northeast border. It would be here any minute.

Rhett squinted upriver and bent his ear to the wind. Beaver barks sounded from a distance. At least the large rodents were useful for something other than making river messes. The newcomers to Sanchia had caused havoc in the creeks ever since they had arrived from the north. Did they really need that many dams and lodges? He could still hear Saloma's admonition to be patient with them while they learn Sanchia's ways. She would at least be happy to know he'd found a way for the beavers to contribute.

A sharp call from Azul alerted Rhett, and he turned his focus again upstream. But he couldn't see any change. He was about to shoot Azul a questioning look when a swirl from the brown below caught his attention. Fattima, the anaconda, lurked just below the creek surface.

"She's going to disrupt the shipment!" Rhett hissed to Azul. "The beavers are skittish anyway about this whole business. We've gotta get rid of her!"

"Now, why would you be ssso unwelcoming, Prophet, to your loyal sssubject?" The voice Rhett dreaded—the voice that sent shivers down his tail—the voice dripping with sarcasm floated up from the waters like an awful apparition.

Rhett shook even though he hated the thought of letting Fattima know of the colony of ants racing up his spine. He took a deep breath and returned. "You loyal? Not even close."

Fattima slithered out of the water and spiraled her way up Rhett's tree trunk. She smirked between tongue flicks. "Did you enjoy your little sssnake hunt the other night? It was all rather exciting."

A massive cloud floated by at just that moment, blocking the sunlight. What had been a bright afternoon now darkened as if a storm approached. Fattima crept onto his branch, her massive weight bending it so low that his tail bobbed on the water's surface.

"I hope you don't mind if I share your perch. I do enjoy a nice view."

Panic seeped into Rhett's mind. He stammered, "A-a-a nice view of what?"

How does she know? Only the head elders knew a shipment was due—only a few of them would have known exactly when.

"Oh, come now, Rhett."

"Prophet, if you please." Rhett interrupted, her blatant disregard for his title pushing him past personal fears.

"Fine, Prophet, if you care to be formal. You should know by now that I rule these watersss. Nothing happensss here without my consssent. You may think you rule Sanchia, but the watersss are mine."

"That's where you're wrong, Fattima. The Sovereign entrusted all Sanchia to my care: land and creek."

Fattima snorted, causing the branch to shake and even more of his tail to get wet. "The Sovereign? Blah. There's no such person— just a made up being to sssatisfy weak-minded animalsss such as yoursssself."

Rhett didn't answer at first. He wasn't sure what to say to such an attack on the Sovereign Himself. Plus, this wasn't a great time for a debate. The beaver barks were getting closer, and he didn't want Fattima around. How could he get rid of this nuisance and defend the Sovereign at the same time?

"Fattima, reason alone is enough to convince any animal of the Sovereign: the Creator, the Sustainer of our jungle. You can't possibly be serious with your ludicrous mockery. You just hate the thought of bowing to Him like you refuse to bow to me."

Fattima twitched, and both recognized it for what it was.

"That's it, isn't it? You know there's a Sovereign, you just refuse to serve Him."

The giant snake jerked her head to face Rhett. When she saw the fear flash across his face, she relaxed her posture and resumed her sly smile.

"I give allegianccce to one greater than the Sovereign, one who understandsss and sssympathizes with the sssnakes' lot. I will never bow to another."

Rhett stared—shocked silent by the snake's profession. He hadn't heard of anyone even coming close to that measure of disrespect. Before he could think of a sensible retort, the beaver lodge came into view.

Not an actual beaver lodge—it was an idea Rhett had developed to transport the purchased goods downriver. The beavers helped construct a log platform and covered it much like they would one of their homes. However, this "lodge" had no anchor and would float easily along the river. Beavers on either side steered the barge and hid it among the reeds if they needed a rest or if trouble came.

The shipment was in full view now, about two palm tree lengths out. Fattima stuck her nose straight in the air as if trying to crack her back. Rhett was torn between watching her and the barge.

How can I get her away from here? She'll only make trouble. We'll have enough to worry about getting the food hauled to the Wimba.

The supplies would be stored at the Sanctuary for safekeeping until it could be fairly distributed to the neediest gatherers. Rhett was about to call for Azul to stall the pack animals from arriving while Fattima was near when the bark of the beavers stopped. It was an eerie silence after the last few minutes of constant beaver chanting.

In the silence, Fattima spoke. "One more shocker for you, Rhett. The prophet'ssscurssse is ssstrong enough to only delay the inevitable. I will choossse the day of your death and mine. I dream of the day when I will sssqueeze the very life from your lungs. Oh, the intenssse joy I'll have when I ssswallow you whole."

Rhett didn't have a chance to respond even if he could have thought of something worth saying. Hundreds of monkeys, maybe more, dropped into view and hung silently by one arm from branches on both sides of the creek. Their gazes fixed on the barge.

They know! Before he could even think to warn the beavers, the monkeys swung in unison onto the barge or into the surrounding waters. The biggest of them tore into the wooden disguise while others countered the small measure of resistance from the beavers. When it was apparent that the barge was taken, the beavers dove deep and didn't resurface.

"Stop!" yelled Rhett. "It's not yours—it's for the orphans, the needy, the desperately hungry."

The monkeys either didn't hear or didn't care. They ripped off the top layer of the lodge revealing piles of nuts, seeds, mangoes, bananas, etc.

"The desssperately hungry, Rhett?" laughed Fattima. "I'd say these monkeyssss are both desssperate and hungry." She began to hum an eerie melody that reminded him of midnight herons as she untangled herself from the branch.

"You did this, didn't you?" Rhett questioned the departing snake. "How'd you know?"

Fattima stuck her pointed nose a paws length from Rhett's chin. Was he imagining it or did her eyes take on a reddish hue? In a high-pitched voice, she hissed. "I know all, Rhett."

She laughed again while creeping backward into the murky water. "I would ssstay and watch the monkeys enjoy themselves, but the ssscene has understandably made me hungry." At the last second, before going under, she hissed, "Now where did those beavers swim off to?"

Rhett couldn't take his eyes off the departing snake as she disappeared beneath the brown eddies. By the time he turned his attention back to the shipment, the monkeys had completely swarmed the barge. The make-shift raft dipped precariously in and out of the muddy waters. He tried hollering again. "Stop, get off. The seeds, the nuts, they'll be ruined." Even though he yelled until he was hoarse, not one monkey even acknowledged his presence.

Defeated, he slumped back on the branch and watched as the monkeys stuffed their mouths with fruit and danced on the sinking barge.

Discussion Questions

1. What would you say to someone who believed that God was a made-up fairy tale figure?

2. Do you think people have trouble admitting that they believe in God because if they did, then they would have to do what He says?

Chapter

06

Tribal Trouble

"**G**rrr!" The vibrating roar of an angry jaguar rebounded off the walls of Giran's cave, waking him from a midnight nap. He tensed, and pain shot through his lower hip reminding him of his wound.

Is Cora in danger?

The hissing and grunting of countless other jaguars joined the first in an enraged cat chorus. He gritted his teeth and pushed up on his three good legs. Limping to the cave opening, he got his first glimpse of the settlement. Even though only a tiny crescent of a moon shed light on the plateau, his sharp eyes adjusted and scanned the horizon for both Cora and the source of danger.

The area in front of his cave was level ground, a spacious courtyard of jungle grass intermixed with patches of dirt. The dirt patches were under scattered shade trees, and most likely formed by romping cubs and resting mamas. About five palm tree lengths from his cave, the terrain dropped off drastically and dipped out of sight. If Giran squinted, he could see where the land reappeared on the horizon as another steep mountain slope. Shadows moved along the adjacent hillsides, and some of the darker patches were not shadows at all but more caves like the one he was in.

The sounds were growing frantic, and in the midst was a jaguar's urgent scream of pain. Though Giran looked every which way, he could not see the fighting that occurred in the brush and the pathways connecting the numerous caves along the mountainside borders.

In the courtyard, young cubs were gathered and sheltered by mamas whose eyes, like Giran's, kept sweeping the perimeter.

"There's Cora," Giran whispered in relief. She was in the center of the field, hovering over four or five young cats. *Is she a Mama already? She's too young. She never said anything.*

A movement from the inner right corner of the courtyard drew his attention away from Cora. Out of a pass between two mountains, a large jaguar bounded into the open at full speed. He headed for the females as they frantically gathered the cubs in a protective bundle at the center. "Why is a warrior attacking cubs?" Giran shouted—no one was listening.

The females ushered up a cacophony of warning calls, and four other large cats emerged from the woods from various locations. They raced to form a barrier between the charging cat and the huddled group of innocents.

The attacker saw the futility. Even though he appeared to be well endowed with muscle and speed, he was no match for four opposing warriors. He skidded to a stop leaving behind a furrowed trail in the grass. With a show of anger and defiance, he leaned back on his haunches and roared.

The other fighting sounds ceased at the roar along with normal jungle noise like the birds and distant screams of the monkeys. It was so quiet that the panting of the warriors on the field could be heard from fifty tail lengths away.

When the lone jaguar came back to all fours, he scanned the camp, daring any warrior to a one-on-one challenge. He had no offers. When his head turned Giran's way, their eyes met, and recognition flashed like lightning.

"Adan." Giran gasped and slowly backed into the shadows of his cave. But it was too late. He had been seen.

The four warriors on the field moved in sync toward Adan in a silent demonstration that he had better leave. His brother gave one of his characteristic half grins toward Giran's cave, full of sarcasm and disgust, then turned and ran off the sloped edge into the darkness.

***

Giran lay at the entry of his cave the rest of the evening, watching the others mill about the courtyard. Some of the other cats noticed his vigilance, but if they thought anything of it, they showed no signs. He especially watched the cubs. Normally young ones were rambunctious by nature, but these were calm, not daring to stray from the safety of their surrounding elders.

Also strange was that all the cubs were female. Giran thought about that for some time but couldn't come up with any explanation. Maybe he'd ask Cora about it later.

The beautiful jaguar—and her litter of kits—was another conundrum that had him wide awake until sunrise. All her female cubs looked to be several seasons old. *How can Cora be their mother? She barely looks older than some of them.*

He pondered these things alongside his relationship with his brother. How he wished things would have gone the other way with Adan. He longed for a family, and Adan was his brother, well, half-brother. But still, there was a blood connection. If Tirgato would have drawn them together—they could have been close—could have been brothers in the truest of senses. But their father had known only hate and lust for power.

By mid-morning, Giran was fretting that Cora might not come. He wanted water, but it was his thirst for her companionship that he relished. *Will she take the time to lick my wound today?* He wished he could groom her in return, but he didn't dare without her father's permission.

He had about given up and was ready to doze when he heard two sets of paw steps coming toward the cave from the far left. Both cats appeared together in the entryway. Cora carried a coconut shell full of water that she deposited next to Giran's mat.

"Good morning," greeted Cora in a softer and shyer tone than usual.

Accompanying her was an enormous jaguar. He stood two paw lengths above Cora with a massive head that, if held high enough, would graze the cave ceiling. He had graying fur, and the many whiskers framing his square jaw swayed in the breeze like a patch of seeding dandelions.

"Giran, this is my father and head of our clan, Elder Ramiro."

Giran struggled to stand up—to properly greet this elder—but the jaguar raised his enormous paw. "Please, no. Lie still and rest. Here, I'll lie with you." Elder Ramiro circled and stretched out toward the opening beside Giran. Cora followed suit but angled herself so they could converse in a semicircle.

The older jaguar started to speak, but no words came. He stared at Giran's side, mouth still open as if the words got lodged behind his teeth.

Is he worried about my injury? It's my leg—not my side. Should I mention that? The shadows on the floor crept by while the elder just stared. Giran thumped his tail to fill the awkward silence. When it became too uncomfortable, Giran said, "Sir, it's getting better every day. Nothing to worry about. I ..."

Ramiro's head jerked up to meet Giran's gaze. "No, I wasn't thinking about that. Forgive me for my rudeness." He lowered his head in the customary sign of contrition.

Giran quickly remarked, "Nothing to forgive, sir, nothing."

Cora's father raised his head and looked straight into the younger jaguar's eyes. "Your markings, they intrigue me." Another pause, and the elder stared out of the cave deep in thought.

Giran didn't try to rush him but looked over at Cora. Her wide eyes and tilted head showed she was just as puzzled as he.

"Your markings. They are the same as a young cub I knew seasons ago, a young jaguar who was my cousin's female cub. She was a beauty. My cousin, though, was a hard jaguar, a fool if you ask me. He cared about nothing but himself, no concern even for his daughter. Anyway, she had the same three-dot pattern on her side that you show. It's a rather rare pattern, thus … it puzzles me."

Giran had no idea what to say to this piece of information, from a stranger no less.

Cora broke the silence, "Father, what was her name, this beautiful jaguar?"

"Raissa. Raissa was her name."

Discussion Questions

1. Why is having brothers and sisters so special and a part of God's good design for us as members of a family?

2. If you don't have a brother or sister, who are some people in your life who can help fill these roles?

Chapter

07

Walking with the Wicked

The bloated belly of Elder Mateo reflected off the surface of the water as big and as bright as a dry season full moon. The hefty spider monkey sat on a dead branch that had fallen and bridged a corner of the pool. He had been there for a while, scratching himself while peering nervously around.

"Maybe he'ssss looking for help," Fattima chuckled under her breath. "He'sss at least sssmart enough to ssstay out of reach. Of course, it would be comical if he happened to lossse his balance and tip into my watersss. Would I sssave him, I wonder?"

The anaconda swallowed the notion with an empty gulp and swam to the beach. If she were to enact sweet revenge, cause havoc for the upstart Prophet, and live in freedom, she needed at least some assistance—for now.

"Elder Mateo," she hissed as she emerged from the water, "ssso nice to have you visit."

The monkey glanced her way with disdain and then looked away—again scanning the surrounding area.

The pompous, overweight primate. He should be groveling and thanking me right now. But instead of venting her true thoughts, she breathed deep through her flaring nostrils. "Don't worry, Elder Mateo. No one elssse is here. I am very adept at ensssuring the upmossstprivacccy."

True enough, the small pool she had claimed for herself was at the end of one of Sanchia's many tributaries. Its out-of-the-way location helped ensure separation from any larger animals not otherwise deterred by her voluminous appetite. If new or uninformed creatures did happen upon her little haven, the signs of anaconda were easy to recognize. If she was there, vibrations tremored the surface of the small still waters, shaking even the nearby fronds. If she wasn't home, her tell-tale markings would be drawn in the muddy banks.

All in all, the pool was Fattima's own exclusive jungle resort—suiting her purposes and whims. It was deep enough to allow for temperature comfort and boasted an easy-to-access beach area for occasional sunning. Of course, there were always the frogs and smaller fish that slightly annoyed her and provided the occasional snack. But mainly she allowed them to stay because they served to keep the pool from turning altogether septic. During the drought, the water level had dipped, and the algae was becoming a nuisance the fish couldn't even keep up with.

"Just being cautious, Fattima, can't be too cautious. This jungle has ears."

Fattima slithered out of the water and straightened her long body out on the dry sand. She didn't want to appear aggressive yet couldn't resist showing off her extended length, the size of a small palm tree. She said in her sweetest voice, "Very wissse of you, Elder. Dissscretion is an admirable trait for a jungle leader. Pity it's also one of the raressst."

Mateo stared at her with a cocked head. The orange tuft of hair on his head—which strongly resembled some bizarre type of caterpillar—looked as if it was teetering on the edge of a cliff.

Ha, Fattima snorted. *He's confused, the sssimpleton. He'll ssserve me well.* After letting him stew a bit, Fattima asked, "Did you enjoy your feassst yesterday?"

"Oh, yes. Of course, Fattima. Many thanks for letting us know about the barge. My young monkeys have scarcely had a good meal in seasons."

Letting the conversation lull, Fattima studied the sweat dripping off the old monkey into the still water below. Perhaps she should offer him a cool dip in her pond. The thought distracted her.

Elder Mateo cleared his throat. "I was just getting ready to send you word of our appreciation when your messenger came."

Fattima nodded her massive head. "Don't worry a flick of the tongue about thanksss. It was thanks enough to see your young onesss enjoying the treatsss. I hope you were able to partake. I didn't see you there?"

"Oh, well, my nephews brought me plenty. I didn't want to be ..."

Fattima knew exactly why Mateo didn't want to be there. He didn't want to take the heat from Rhett. *He'll plead ignorance when confronted by the kinkajou, which is closer to the truth than he realizes.*

Fattima cleared her throat and dug deep for a tone of compassion. "Don't you get tired of anssswering to a Prophet, Mateo? Wouldn't you like to rule your clansss without interferencece?"

Mateo jerked his head around to peer into the surrounding dark jungle brush. Fattima knew he was no lover of the Prophet system— he was a great lover of his own hide.

"I-I'm not sure th-this is healthy co-co-conversation, Fattima. We-we've always had a P-P-Prophet. It se-seems to work."

Fattima shook her tail. "But, Elder, I have traveled to many regionsss along the waterwaysss. There are regionsssswhossse Prophet is barely known and even regionsss without one."

Mateo repositioned on his branch to better face Fattima. "How? How do they ..."

Fattima interrupted. "How do they do what? Rule their own affairs? Make judgments based on the needsss of their own offspring." Fattima huffed and flared her nostrils. "They know bessst what their familiesss need, and they do well. What hasss a Prophet ever done for you that you couldn't have done yoursssself? There'sss another way, Mateo, a better way."

The elder scratched another bald spot off his belly, and his eyes were squinted almost shut. One side of his ugly face pulled tight into a grimace. The head pain must be taxing considering his unusual task of thinking. In desperation, Mateo finally spit out, "I can't disagree with you. I have wondered…"

"I knew you mussst have wondered, Elder. Your heart mussst beat like mine for independenccce, for freedom from the rule of animalsss who can't understand the needsss of your family."

"But, Fattima …" Mateo warned in a hushed tone. "This is dangerous talk. We could be heard."

Fattima inched a little closer to the elder's perch. "What if I told you that Sanchia is clossse to freedom, clossser than the whisssskers on your chin."

Elder Mateo squinted again. *He's ssslow but nibbling at the bait.* Fattima held back a satisfied hiss of amusement. "Are you truly happy, Elder? Are your familiesss thriving?"

Mateo shook his head. "We're stretched thin, for sure."

The elder's bulging midsection did not give the appearance of being stretched thin. As a matter of fact, the tempting sight made Fattima's dorsal muscles spontaneously contract.

The monkey continued, "What are you talking about here? What can be done to get this independence?"

"Very little, Mateo. That'sss the beauty of it. You do very little of what Rhett asksss. Sssooner or later, when that happensss, and like I said, I've ssseen it elsewhere. SSSooner or later, with no one lissstening, the Prophet just stopsss commanding."

"Hmm." murmured the elder. "I'll give this some thought, Fattima. I surely will."

"In the meantime, Mateo, I need a little favor. One to ssshow your appreciation for the feassstyesssterday and to sssseal our mutual partnership. That is if you would like future asssssistance? The monkeys are a powerful clan, and with my ssskills and knowledge, we could make formidable allies."

The ancient monkey took a moment to study the stars. He had a pleasing look on his face that spread with the mention of the monkey's power. "I agree, Fattima. A partnership would benefit us both. Ummm, what do you need?"

"I desssire the sssachet of medicccinalherbsss that the Prophet hordesss in hisss tree. I'm regrettably too ssslow on land to gather the herbsss myself."

"He'd probably just give you some of them if you asked. My young ones go there all the time for cuts and scrapes. Wouldn't that be simpler?"

A dark look flashed across Fattima's slits as she coiled into an ominous position. "I will not asssk Rhett for anything. He keepsss the medicccines stored sssomewhere in the Wimba. I need the sssachet that holdsss the red achiote seedsss. There might be more than one. In that case, bring them all. As a matter of fact, if your monkeysss are unsure, tell them to grab them all."

Elder Mateo, deep in thought, leaned to one side and slightly raised a leg. A pungent puff of wind burst free. A few unfortunate flies dropped dead in the water.

Fattima vibrated in frustration. *What is taking the crude creature so long? Swim calm—Fattima—swim calm.* "You know, Elder, your monkeys could be in and out of the Wimba faster than a frog's tongue on a fat fly.

Mateo smiled at the amusing image and the flattering of his kin. "Why do you need the herbs, Fattima? You sick?"

The anaconda laughed. "You don't need to know, Mateo. You don't really want to know, do you? Just get the herbsss to me by moonrissse tomorrow."

Mateo scooted off the branch onto solid land and nodded his head. Fattima knew he would see it her way – knew yesterday's feast and the promise of more would enslave the dumb beast. He would also come around to her way of thinking regarding politics, probably already was—but too scared to admit it.

Mateo lumbered off without a dismissal or even a polite goodbye. "Hmm," muttered the anaconda under her breath. "He won't leave sssoeasssily next time."

"Elder." He called to the monkey's retreating figure. "Don't forget all that we talked about."

The monkey didn't even turn around but shook his head while in retreat. As he reached for an overhanging branch, he muttered, "I'll have a group deliver the herbs to the beach here by sunset tomorrow."

"Delightful." But the words didn't reach the elder. He was already swinging back up the creek, away from Fattima. "Pity he didn't ssstay for dinner," she laughed.

Discusssion Questions

1. Read Psalm 1 (NIV). How does this Psalm apply to the chapter?

> [1] Blessed is the one
> who does not walk in step with the wicked
> or stand in the way that sinners take
> or sit in the company of mockers,
>
> [2] but whose delight is in the law of the Lord,
> and who meditates on his law day and night.
>
> [3] That person is like a tree planted by streams of water,
> which yields its fruit in season
> and whose leaf does not wither—
> whatever they do prospers.
>
> [4] Not so the wicked!
> They are like chaff
> that the wind blows away.
>
> [5] Therefore the wicked will not stand in the judgment,
> nor sinners in the assembly of the righteous.

[6] For the LORD watches over the way of the righteous,
  but the way of the wicked leads to destruction.

2. Is the freedom Fattima seeks a good or bad thing? Why?

Chapter

08

Family Connections

Giran's ears perked, and he raised up on both front legs. "Raissa, are you sure?"

It was Elder Ramiro's time to show surprise. "Yes son, of course I'm sure. The families were close."

Giran silently pleaded for more but was too shocked to think of the right questions. The elder must have realized he was tongue-tied and took pity on the wide-eyed youth. "It was back when I still lived in Cantiga before we resettled here in Altura. I was newly covenanted and excited to start my own family when Raissa disappeared one evening. No one was sure what happened to her, and her father and mother were tight-lipped about the whole ordeal. Most think she followed a newcomer who had been hanging around for a few weeks. But now tell me, why the interest?"

"Raissa was my mother."

The elder raised up on his forelegs to meet Giran's gaze. "Raissa's son. Amazing resemblance now that you mention it." He proceeded to scrutinize every spot pattern on Giran while mumbling, "Amazing resemblance."

Giran felt his tail spring straight up. He tried to at least bring it down to a reasonable height—it was a little embarrassing. But how could he hold back his excitement? He had loved his mother more than anything.

A warm grin spread across the elder's face, and as he chuckled, he issued an invitation. "Can you walk with me, just a little way?"

Giran didn't hesitate, the pain in his leg could be ignored. "Yes, I think so."

"Good." The elder looked out upon the courtyard, and Giran's eyes followed.

The open field was alive with activity. Small and big cubs alike were at play, moms were huddled nearby talking, and the young warriors were having workout fights on the far end.

The elder spoke again. "Come, Raissa's son, let me introduce you to the cats of Altura—many your blood kin."

Giran stood up using his three good legs, and even though he walked with a distinct limp, he was able to follow the elder out of the cave. They walked together down a winding side path and out to the center of the field. Cora came slightly behind them, and when he glanced her way, he saw that she wore a shy grin on her face.

The stares of the now still and watching cats pelted him like drops of first rain. Elder Ramiro lay down in the green grass on a small rise and bid him join. Giran's eyes widened, and he glanced nervously at Cora. The honor did not escape his notice—even if he was raised in a social bubble with a tyrant as a father.

Still favoring his injured leg, Giran carefully stretched out on the warm grass and got his first full view of Cora's home. On three sides were mountain cliffs completely covered with palm trees and lush jungle vegetation. Only on one side did the field appear to drop off. Even from his current vantage, he could not decipher what lay between the dipping slope and the neighboring mountainside.

"So, Raissa's son, is that going to be your name? I doubt you want to be called, 'Raissa's son' forever." He chuckled at his dry humor.

"Giran, sir."

The elder looked kindly at the younger jaguar and then at Cora. "I assume you know that this is Corazón, my oldest cub."

"Your oldest, sir?"

"Yes, oldest of five beautiful cubs: all females. Each more precious than a thousand still pools brimming with fish." The elder playfully swished at Cora with his tail.

Giran slanted his eyes. *Is he being sarcastic? Jaguar fathers only want sons.* But no hint of sarcasm showed on Ramiro's face. Maybe the son thing was another of Tirgato's quirks.

Giran pointed with his nose toward the group of males who had resumed their training not far from where they lay. "Are they family?"

"Oh yes, nephews mostly. But some are cousins of cousins. On occasion I recruit young males from families in Cantiga and Vancíon to settle here. They serve to protect our tribe and will, in time, form family units of their own. Many have already brought in mates and had cubs."

The mention of protection brought the raid back to mind and the image of his brother. Something deep within told him this might not be the best time to make known that particular family connection. "Why do you need protection? Who were the jaguars from last night?"

"They're part of a smaller tribe led by an elder named Vinícius. They also call Altura home. But they're outsiders—have been for seasons. They came here looking for rest and temporary solace, they said. They were just passing through, they said. We showed them every hospitality until it became apparent that they were not just visiting. They intended to stay."

Giran looked at Cora, and though she made the pretense of listening, he could tell she had heard the same story times before. Her tail was gracefully swishing the green grass in a mesmerizing fashion.

He forced his eyes back into focus on her father. Hopefully, the elder had not noticed his diverted attention.

"They wanted to change many of our customs like how and when to hunt, how to train the young ones, work rotations, just strange stuff – not like what we were used to. When they elected elders behind our backs, I knew it was time for them to go. Even though they didn't openly admit it—they wanted control of the region."

Elder Ramiro paused for a moment and stared off into the sloping horizon. Giran prompted, "So what did you do?"

"I recruited some young warriors, and we ran them out before they got too powerful—out of the highlands into the flatter portion of Altura. A massacre wasn't an option—there were some females and cubs. But we made sure they were aware that the highlands were no longer to be shared with them or their offspring."

"Was there enough prey for them in the lowlands?"

"Of course. At first, they did well. Both of our tribes respected the boundaries, and they thrived in the lowlands for many seasons. But lately, they've been stirring up trouble. They covet our females. Only the Sovereign knows why, but the tribe has had male cubs for seasons in abundance and very few females. Personally, I wonder if the females were eradicated at birth."

Ramiro paused to let the gruesome thought permeate. Giran hoped he was wrong.

"Over time, as nature has it, the young males grew up and desired a family. They look to us now to provide the females they lack. But I'll be slaughtered before I see my girls go to that barbarian tribe!"

Ramiro rose then and paced in front of Giran.

"Last night, they raided as a team but targeted only one guard. He's alive but will never fight again. They attack one of our brothers at a time, hoping to weaken us." He scratched at the grass with his paw and added in a quieter tone that couldn't be heard outside their small circle. "It's working—the dishonorable piles of scat."

Giran didn't reply, any words said now would fall flatter than a beaver's tail. He glanced over at Cora instead and forgot whatever the elder was talking about. Her long eyelashes fluttered like a butterfly's wings. He could watch her sleep all evening.

Ramiro stopped his pacing, and Giran detected a quiet chuckle beside him. He had been caught admiring the elder's beautiful daughter. His face turned the color of a baboon's behind.

When Ramiro spoke, Cora roused from her slumber. "Cora, I need to check on the injured scout. And please keep an eye on your sisters."

"Sisters." Giran thought. "They're her sisters." He silently rejoiced.

As the elder strode away, he turned back to address Giran, twinkle still in his eye. "I'm glad you're here, Giran. You're family and welcome to stay."

Giran nodded his thanks and closed his eyes. Ramiro had no idea what those words meant to him—what the prospect of family meant to him. When he opened them again, he saw the old jaguar walking away through a sheen of moisture. He forced the tears back though. He couldn't have his new family think he was an emotional sap.

Discussion Questions

1. Why did Giran relish the feeling of being told by Ramiro that he was family?

2. Take some time to thank God for the family He has given you. How can you express your appreciation to your family?

Chapter

09

The Mystery of the Missing Medicine

The acrid odor filled his nostrils. Smoke again. Third day in a row. *Where is this dream coming from?* Sometimes it was so heavy in the air when he awoke that he feared the Wimba was in danger. He had asked Azul about it the day before, sure that someone besides him would have seen the smoke. But Azul reported only heavy fog over the area—nothing so thick and black as smoke.

One would think I'd have normal nightmares like starvation, sickness, being eaten or caged—normal kinkajou dreams. But no, I have dreams that may or may not come true and leave me stressed and confused.

Rhett crawled down to the Wimba platform. He had a few moments before the Council began. Of course, not enough time to come up with a solution to the food shortage or think of an explanation for what happened with the food that was supposed to be here for distribution. *So many will be disappointed.*

Rhett dangled his legs over the platform edge while watching several of the early elders appear along the fringe of the Sanctuary. Upon seeing him on the platform, the animals gathered. The Prophet scanned the faces, looking for Mateo. He had sent word by Azul to have the elder meet him privately before the Council, but the old monkey had yet to show.

Why did he take the food meant for the needy? Mateo's contrary but not evil-mean like others— Fattima for example. Is Mateo taking sides with her?

It wouldn't do any good to publicly call the monkeys out anyway. To the other hungry animals, it would just sound like another excuse. No, he wouldn't win any favors by placing the blame on anyone else. He should have kept it a better secret—should have protected the shipment somehow.

When the animals had all assembled, Elder Horado led the scarcer-than-normal group through the initial proceedings. During the role and pledge known as the Oración, most of the beavers elbowed their way to the front, no doubt eager to hear all the details of the botched barge fiasco. Besides the beavers, the gathering of elders included deer, birds of all sizes and colors, agouti, armadillo, squirrels, bush dogs, capybara, kinkajous, peccary, otters, tapirs, turtles, and most noticeably, no monkeys.

Where are they? Rhett shook his head in frustration. All the elders were commanded to be in Council attendance if healthy. *Now I have to deal with their absence at Council on top of the barge supply theft?*

The Council preliminaries were soon completed. The creatures raised their eyes to the platform, ready for Rhett to speak, to explain the news many of them had already heard along the jungle vines. They didn't really want to hear the story again, they wanted hope, they wanted to hear the, 'What I'm Going to Do Next Speech.' *Shoot, I want to hear the, 'What I'm Going to Do Next Speech'.*

Rhett had just opened his mouth to blunder some nonsense about patience when a young marsh deer burst out of the east side of the Sanctuary borders. On open field, the deer raced, kicking up a cloud of dust large enough to choke half the critters in Sanchia.

"Prophet, Prophet," he huffed as he drew closer to the Wimba. The crowd parted for the young buck as he slowed to a trot. Sweat ran like streams, creating striped patterns down the side of his crusted hide.

"Prophet, come quick. Tomás is hurt bad. The bees ..." he paused to suck in air while the crowd leaned in. "The bees weren't dead. See we thought they waz dead. Tomás crushed the hive with his hoof so we could get us some honey. We thought they waz dead. They didn't sing any, and we ate up. I went to drink, and Tomás waz still eating. But then they started to sing loud, very loud, and attacked Tomás. He waz covered before I could holler – before I could think straight. He ran into the creek like a mad boar, and most of the bees took off. But Tomás, he's bad off now. He's just lying by the creek. He won't get up, Prophet. You gotta come quick."

Rhett, knowing the problem, sent up a prayer of thanks for Saloma's extensive training. *All those mind-dumbing days at school were helpful after all. Who'd have thought?*

Rhett raced up the Wimba to the place where they had always stored the medicine. He knew exactly which one would combat the swelling caused by the bees—the achiote seeds. *Good thing we keep a few of them stored away; there's not a blooming achiote fruit in this whole region.* Every creature loved the bright red fruit, but few realized that the crushed and dried seeds could be of even greater value if needed.

In the upper region of the Wimba where two main branches converged like a snake's tongue, there was a good-sized hole. The opening was bigger than a standard kinkajou nook so whereas he could crawl into the storage compartment, Saloma had always had to reach her paw in to find the medicines. Because of her limitations, she made sure that the nook stayed organized and as neat as any ant colony. The achiote would be in the back left corner opposite the enticing medicinal honeycombs. He drooled just thinking of the honeycombs.

Come on, Rhett. Focus! He shook his head and dove into the nook headfirst. His eyes adjusted while his breath stopped. The entire nook was empty. Only a drop of crusted honey littered the bare floor.

Rhett turned around several times hoping with each revolution that the precious medicine would reappear. If it wasn't for the dab of honey, he would have suspected that he had the wrong nook—the wrong tree even. But there weren't many storage compartments in the Wimba, and he knew this was the one for medicines. *What am I going to do? Tomás needs the achiote!*

Rhett scrambled out of the nook and all the way to the ground. Elder Horado, the elder of the marsh deer community, pawed at the grass, watching Rhett's every move. The kinkajou ran over to Elder Horado. "Elder, there's no medicine. Everything's gone in the medicinal nook."

The marsh deer stopped his pawing—his ears perked to the heavens. "What do you mean gone? Where's the medicine?"

Every ounce of Rhett shook. "I don't know. The nook was fully stocked last time I checked. Now it's empty—I have no idea what happened."

"Well, what do you need for Tomás?" Elder Horado questioned while glancing toward the tree line, muscles taut. "Where can we get more medicine?"

"Tomás needs the achiote seeds."

Elder Horado's head jerked back to meet Rhett's stare full-on. "The achiote! There's no achiote left."

Rhett hung his head and moaned. He couldn't bear to witness the horror registering in the elder deer's face. *What would Saloma do? I wish she was here instead of me.*

When Elder Horado turned to sprint off, Rhett reached for his leg. "Take me to him, Elder. You can fly faster than I through the marsh. Maybe – I don't know what – but maybe there's something I can still do."

Without another word, the marsh deer bent his head low, and Rhett climbed on. The deer's back muscles were already tight, waiting to be released in full power. Paulo, Tomás' friend, watched for the elder's nod. When the slight movement came, he turned abruptly to lead the way. The crowd, who had been watching the drama unfold

56

with great interest, parted for the two deer and one kinkajou. The other elders would certainly follow but from a respectful distance.

Paulo and Elder Horado sped through the jungle like a gust of wind before a storm. Rhett's knuckles glared white as he gripped the thick fur around Horado's neck. Though the race was harrowing, his thoughts were running wilder than the deer. *Why is this happening? Who took the medicine? How can I help Tomás? Oh, what would Saloma do?*

Discussion Questions

1. Do you agree with Rhett blaming himself for the botched barge incident?

2. To what point does a leader take responsibility for setbacks, especially if the problems were caused by the failures of teammates?

10

Caimans, Confessions, and Confusion

C anopy-colored lily pads blanketed the slow-moving creek. Giran knew it was a bizarre notion, but the lily pads looked to him like a horde of capricious moons that had dropped to earth to hide his prey. They were still now, and he let out a breath. Typically, the pads bobbed just before the black caiman surfaced. The creek monster would appear again soon—he couldn't stay underwater for very long.

He and Cora had crouched in the reeds since sundown. The two of them had been hunting together for the last week, and while hunting with another jaguar was a strange experience, he had thoroughly enjoyed their evening adventures. The idea had been hers. She said it would be a means of regaining his health while still feasting on fresh meat.

Is that her only reason? He had little experience with female jaguars. She had crouched beside him during the long waits versus a more spread-out angled formation. Giran didn't think it wise to point out that logistical flaw.

He glanced over at her. She was focused on the surface of the water, just as he had been seconds before. *Wow, she has a jaw shaped just like the curving of the lily pad flower. I wonder if her fur feels as silky as the pink petals.*

She must have felt his eyes on hers because she glanced his way through graceful, dipping eyelashes. Their gazes connected, and the jungle around him floated away. By the time she broke the connection, more beads of sweat flowed down his neck than droplets of water in the creek.

He murmured under his breath. "I hope that caiman appears soon. I need a dip."

Thankfully, the two didn't have to wait much longer. A stirring in the pads preceded the appearance of a narrow strip of reptile flesh. Its complicated color pattern blended with both the brown water and the dark green algae that floated between lily pads.

Cora's muscles tensed, and Giran felt the tip of her tail brush his. *Was that an accident, a signal, a sign of some kind?* The brief touch broke his concentration. When Cora sprang, he lagged a full jump behind.

She made short work of the caiman, and before Giran could help much, she was dragging him on shore.

"That was great work, Cora. He's a beauty! He'll feed us and your whole family besides."

Cora's mouth was occupied, but she grunted her agreement. Giran took hold of the large reptile's tail and helped tug him the rest of the way.

"Whew." Cora said, collapsing on the sand next to the still flapping caiman. "He was old, but he sure had some fight left in him."

"I thought the wait was more exhausting." Giran smiled.

Cora swept the surface of the beach with her tail, spraying Giran with sand.

"Ugg." Giran playfully whined. "Now I'm going to have to get wet again."

"Did you ever get wet to start with?" She teased.

Giran grinned and went for a short dip while Cora started her supper. Giran waited by the shore until she was done and asked something that he had been wondering about.

"Cora, why do you hunt for your sisters? They're old enough, aren't they?" Giran walked over to enjoy his portion of dinner while she answered.

"The other tribe, you know the jaguars who attacked last week, they're interested in our caves—very interested. But like my father also mentioned, they're after female jaguars. That's the other reason I asked you to hunt with me. Your recovery yeah, but Father also prefers that I don't go by myself. He's adamant that my younger sisters don't go at all."

"I can understand the jaguars wanting mates. But I've never heard of jaguars kidnapping their females?"

"They've tried before, twice in fact. Both times, my father and cousins were able to fight them off."

Giran let that simmer while he finished the tasty morsel he had been working on. Cora sat by the bank grooming herself.

"Cora?"

"Yeah?"

"Why don't you want to go with them—the males I mean? Surely you want a family too."

Cora looked up at him, surprise in her eyes.

Giran looked back at his meal, sorry he had asked such a personal question. "I'm sorry, it's not any of my business."

"No," she answered quietly, "I don't mind."

She didn't speak again for a moment, and Giran tried to respect the silence. But his chewing was louder than a horde of angry howler monkeys.

"My family, well my dad, doesn't want me to find a partner outside the clan. He keeps saying that he'll send one of the cousins back to Cantiga for a suitable mate, but it never seems to be the right time. I wonder if it will ever be the right time."

Cora's eyes were downcast—her shoulders slumped like a day-old-picked flower.

"Why don't you go then, find a mate in another territory?"

Cora looked up in surprise. "I couldn't leave my family. Father needs my help, with my sisters, with the tribe." Looking up at Giran, she added, "My sisters can be quite the pawful."

Giran chuckled at her light comment. "I'm sure they can if they take after their older sister."

Cora sauntered over again, and they both picked at a few more pieces of choice caiman in companionable silence. When Giran spoke, his quiet voice vibrated like a warbling tanager. "Cora, I'm from the same place the other jaguars are originally from—from Sanchia."

"I know, silly." She answered without even glancing his way. "Have known from the beginning. You have the same accent."

Giran squinted his eyes. He didn't realize he had an accent.

"But don't worry about that." She smiled. "You're not like them. You're honorable. Father says it's his family's blood that runs strong through your veins."

Giran savored that statement more than the caiman he just ate. These were Raissa's kin—his family. He belonged with them, and he fit in for once in his life. He started his after-dinner grooming with more satisfaction than usual.

On the way back to the caves, the two took turns dragging the extra caiman meat. But even if they didn't have dinner to haul, they wouldn't have talked. Both were absorbed in their thoughts. Giran's head swelled with dreams of evenings to come—with cubs and friends and fun.

As they approached the edge of the field, Cora's sisters ran to greet them. Forgetting their manners, they tore into the offered meat. The next oldest, Sofia, chided them. "What took you two so long? We're starving!"

The innocent enough phrase cut Giran like a sharpened claw. Rhett was waiting, the animals of Sanchia were waiting—starving—

and here he was well fed and content. Giran moaned, and his ears and tail flattened.

"What's wrong, Giran?" Cora asked. "Sofia didn't mean anything, she's just impatient."

Sofia heard her name and looked up from her meal with an apologetic half smile on her face. "Sorry, Giran. Thanks for the caiman. You too, Cora." Having satisfied herself with niceties, she returned to her supper.

"Cora, it wasn't that. It's ..." and he trailed off. *How can I tell her?*

Cora turned her head to one side and flicked him with her tail. "It's what Giran? What's got you upset? You seemed happy before— your tail waved tall most of the way home."

"Ahhh. Cora, I'm not here to stay. In Altura, I mean. I'm leaving soon to go back to Sanchia. I have to go back."

Her eyes opened wide. "Why, Giran? Why not stay here with us? You belong here."

"I made a pact with my best friend—kinkajou. I told him I'd return with some jaguars to help Sanchia."

A deep voice chimed in from behind the two. "A kinkajou? Wiry little creatures—don't care for the taste."

Both turned towards Cora's father, who had come over to take part in the offered dinner.

Giran studied his paws, hesitant to address Elder Ramiro. He hated to tell them this way, but he had to. He couldn't just disappear one day without an explanation.

"Yes, my best friend is a kinkajou named Rhett."

Both Cora and her father wrinkled their noses, but it was her father who asked. "So, you weren't out looking for a mate?"

"No, not really. Not for a mate—for a group of jaguars to come with me back to Sanchia."

The elder stared at the caiman and his daughters enjoying the feast but made no other move toward the meal. His jaw clenched shut. "Son, I don't understand all you're after, but if you've come to take my family back to some backward jungle away from me, you're in the wrong place. Now, stop thinking about that foolishness and look around. We have all you need here. A family, a mate, a real opportunity to live the best life a jaguar could hope for."

Giran shook his head. "You don't understand. The animals—the gatherers—in Sanchia are starving. They've populated so much without the cats in the jungle that there's not enough to eat. They need jaguars to come to restore the balance. I promised Rhett."

This time, Ramiro snorted. "A kinkajou, gatherers? You're concerned about kinkajous?"

Giran tilted his head. *How can I get him to understand?* Then it dawned on him what he'd missed. "The kinkajou is the Prophet."

"Yeah, yeah. We have one of those too—for what good he is."

It was Giran's turn to stare wide-eyed at the elder jaguar. Ramiro took the silence to mean Giran was considering his words.

"Now we appreciate the offer. I'm sure the hunting is fine in Sanchia. But we have our caves, see, our home, our family. We're not separating. But come son, come and join us."

Giran looked over at Cora, who had been watching the exchange with the same intensity that she had watched the caiman earlier. He wanted to say yes with every one of his jaguar spots. He loved Rhett, but he couldn't say the same for the rest of Sanchia. He had never really fit in there. But, here, here he could be happy and have everything he ever wanted.

Ramiro turned toward the rapidly disappearing caiman, and Cora back to her cave. The conversation was over.

Wait! He wanted to scream but didn't. *I didn't say, 'no.' Why didn't I tell them, 'no'?*

Discussion Questions

1. Elder Ramiro told Cora that it was his family blood running through Giran's veins that made him honorable. Do you agree with that sentiment? Where does the Bible say honor comes from?

2. Have you ever experienced a time when something you wanted to do conflicted with what you needed to do?

Chapter

11

Deer, Death, and Despair

The marsh grass grew so tall alongside Belo Creek that Elder Horado was practically swimming through the blades. Judging from the sloshy sound of his steps, they were traveling the indistinguishable area between creek and dry land. From Rhett's vantage point on Horado's neck, he judged that Paulo was leading them to an opening in the grass ahead—a beach oasis amid the marsh.

Two honey buzzards were flying low—in and out of the clearing—and a family of skunks were gathered around a dark figure lying on the sand. Skunks were notoriously curious, but the buzzards were here for either the honey or Tomás. *Let's hope they only get leftover honey.*

When Horado's step sounded firm, Rhett slipped off his back and scampered toward the sick deer. The alarmed buzzards squawked at the intrusion and veered away from the beach only far enough to perch on an overlooking branch. They were staking their claim to the forthcoming meal. Rhett gave both buzzards a withering look before turning his attention to Tomás.

Rhett placed his paw on Tomás' chest. With his touch, Tomás stirred and moaned. His face was so swollen that he couldn't open his eyes.

"Peace, Tomás. This is the Prophet. You need to lie still and rest." His words were heard, but the meaning must have been distorted because Tomás began to thrash around spewing mud and broken pieces of reed grass into the air.

"Still, Tomás." Rhett commanded, to no avail. Tomás tried to get to all fours but tripped in weakened clumsiness. The deer collapsed back into the mud, wheezing and trembling from the tip of his snout to the tip of his tail.

Rhett scanned his memories for any recollection of how to help a sick animal in this condition, but all he could come up with was the right answer—the achiote seeds.

Elder Horado appeared by Rhett's side along with Paulo and the other elders that had followed from the Wimba. Paulo came over and whispered to his friend, "It's okay, Tomás. Prophet's here now. You're going to be okay."

Tomás turned to his friend's voice. He opened his mouth like he wanted to say something, but only a hoarse and scratchy moan came out.

Rhett kept wracking his mind, hoping for an answer. Maybe he'd missed something. But the more he brooded, the more muddled his thoughts became.

Tomás jerked, focusing Rhett's attention. A flicker of hope shone through Rhett's mind. *This is a good sign.* But when the jerk ended, Tomás lay still, too still. Hope was drowned by a surge of anger. No reasoning lay behind the anger even though if he had thought about it, he could have directed it toward whoever had stolen the achiote. At the moment, though, he was just angry at death.

The anger was fleeting, almost instantly replaced by the weightier feeling of guilt. Rhett had no problem recognizing who to place that emotion on – himself. He was the Prophet; he was responsible for keeping the medicines. He was responsible for the life of Tomás.

Rhett rested his paw on Tomás' side—completely still. Looking up, he met Elder Horado's eyes and shook his head.

Seeing the exchange between the Prophet and his elder, Paulo sank to his knees in the soft sand. He quivered with sobs while the gathering of onlookers stared.

Rhett shook his head in frustration. He could have saved him. The achiote seeds would still have worked. There would have been time. *"Where are the seeds? Why would anyone steal achiote seeds?* Then a new thought dawned. *How does a marsh deer get hold of a beehive?*

Remembering the bees, he looked up in alarm.

"Where are the bees?" He said first in a frightened whisper, looking around. Then a little louder. "Paulo, where's the hive?" He had to shake the young deer and ask twice, but eventually, the mourning deer nodded over his left shoulder.

About a palm tree length away, a nest the size of a large opossum set on top of some trampled reeds. The bees had reclaimed their displaced home and were frantically crawling in and out of every hive hole.

How? Rhett racked his brain in frustration. *How does a hive that size just fall on its own?*

Rhett looked up and saw the branch where it had recently hung. Tendrils of the honeycomb still clung to the bark. *I've never seen such a thing. Those nests don't move for nothing.*

"Ahem." The elder coughed softly, causing both Paulo and Rhett to turn his way. "I'm going to find Tomás' family. They'll want to know."

The honey buzzards had been joined by friends and were now irreverently squawking their delight at Tomás' misfortune. The elder glanced their way and back at Rhett. "Can you keep them off for a while? Until his parents come."

"Of course." Rhett nodded; glad he could do something at least. "Elder, I'm sorry there were no achiote seeds. I don't know where they would have gone—who would have taken them."

The elder refused to meet his gazeand instead stared out over the creek. "I know you're sorry, Rhett."

Anger, frustration, pride – these welled up inside the kinkajou. "Elder, I know they were there last I checked. I didn't eat them!"

By now, all the animals, including Paulo, were more focused on this discussion than on Tomás.

"On top of that, I don't understand how a beehive just falls to the ground. That just doesn't happen. Believe me, it takes a lot of work to crack one of those hives."

Rhett thought back on the hives he had enjoyed as treats over the years. Honey was a favorite snack for kinkajous but seldom enjoyed by others. It was mostly gathered and used by the Prophets for medicinal purposes or in trading.

"The honey buzzards could have gotten it, but why wouldn't they have eaten the honey if they had taken the time to drop the nest? Why would they leave it on the ground for the deer?"

"Paulo," Rhett asked, "Why'd you go near the hive? Weren't the bees singing?"

Paulo looked at Rhett with wide, wet eyes. "No, Prophet. They were quiet at first, like the dead." His gaze dropped to Tomás with the mention of the word. "We thought they waz dead anyway. We ate our fill—or at least I did—and then I went to get some water from the creek. On my way back is when Tomás started yelping and pawing at the dirt. He ran in circles, crazy-like. I didn't know what waz wrong until I got closer and saw he waz covered in bees. I yelled at him to get in the creek, and he did. But when he got out, he didn't make it but to here and collapsed. That's when I went and got you."

Rhett thought about all that Paulo had told him. When Elder Horado stirred, obviously impatient to fetch Tomás' parents, Rhett asked. "But why were the bees asleep at first?"

He looked at both deer for the answer. He even looked at the two skunks who had been quietly sitting, watching the show. All shrugged ignorance.

Rhett inched forward as close to the fallen hive as he dared go. Then it hit him—hit his nose rather. Yes, there was the scent of honey, the scent of the marsh, the scent of the nearby skunks. But the distinctive sweet odor of ripened fruit also hovered in the air. He hadn't smelled that mouth-watering odor in quite some time—since before the drought. Suspicious, he inched closer to the hive.

On the hive itself—and littering the surrounding marsh grass—were massive amounts of tiny purple grains—the pollen from the Devil's Snare. Rhett hollered over his shoulder to the others who were bent over, straining to see. "This wasn't an accident. This was planned!"

Discussion Questions

1. Have you ever been angry at death?

2. Read 1 Corinthians 15:55-57. Who gives us victory over death?

Chapter

12

Catnapped

Giran peered out onto the open field as shadows from the outlining trees retreated into the jungle. The warm sun glaring off the rock faces of the adjacent cliffs would normally be enough to propel him into a deep sleep. But not today. Cora had gone hunting again without him—probably with some cousin.

Sure, he was capable now of hunting—small game at least. His wound throbbed if he over-exerted, and he knew his strength wasn't back totally. But he could certainly manage to grab something old and slow.

His stomach rumbled, reminding him again of her abandonment. He'd have to hunt at the first sign of evening. An abundance of sloths dwelled in Altura though he couldn't quite get himself to enjoy one considering Saloma's recent death.

Earlier, Cora brought in a large peccary for her family. He'd stayed in the shadows of his cave, not wanting her to know that he had been watching, brooding, waiting for her return. She had been avoiding him ever since their conversation. *Did her Father prohibit them from talking, or does she just not want to have anything to do with me?* The

70

question plagued him. That and the sharp pang of remorse for not standing more firm in his duty to Sanchia. *But how can I be expected to leave her, to leave the family I just found? Surely Rhett would understand?*

As he nursed those thoughts, others flowed in. *I have a responsibility to these jaguars too. They're blood kin. I can't leave them now—not for gatherers who never cared about me anyway. It's foolishness just like Ramiro says.*

A dry twig snapped, breaking into Giran's treacherous thoughts. The drought that had recently hit even the highlands of Altura had made many rare sounds like a dry twig become common. The cats had to adjust to the different ground texture, especially in hunting. *Is Sanchia still being affected by the dry weather? If so, the gatherers are suffering even more.*

Another snap. This one was closer and came from Giran's left. A path ran between dens that wound up and around the mountains that sheltered them. This path, along with other similar winding trails, was used by the jaguars all the time, but not usually at this time of day.

"Who would be moving around in broad daylight?" Giran mumbled. "Curiosity kills the cat."

Unable to resist the pull to investigate, he stood and shook. A change in scenery from the suffocating cave might be just what he needed to clear his head. Wasting no time, he walked into the bright noon shine and took a few quiet leaps along the path he suspected the sound came from. Giran sniffed the ground—Cora and another jaguar whose smell jarred him like dry season thunder.

His muscles tensed—his tail stood straight. By the time his brain registered with his paws, he was already storming up the path. Her scent and the smell of the imposter grew stronger. He heard a muffled yelp. *Why? Why doesn't she scream?*

Like a startled bat, Giran went off-path and charged through the brush to cut off a curve. He emerged from the tangled weeds just behind Cora and her kidnapper. The path was narrow—barely the width of a jaguar—and in danger of being overtaken completely by brush on both sides. Cora walked a few tail lengths away, being prodded forward by nips on her hind end. *Still, she's a strong cat, why not fight or run?*

"Cora!" he yelled as both jaguars turned. Cora showed fear, Adan brimmed with delight.

"Hello, brother," Adan said derisively with half of his mouth turned up. "How nice of you to join us. Out for a noonday stroll? I'm sorry we can't stay and chat, but we're on our way to set up our new den—together."

"Together?" "Brother?" Both Cora and Giran spoke at the same time. Both looked betrayed.

Cora was the first to recover. "I didn't want to, Giran."

Adan issued a low growl. "That's quite enough, Cora."

"No!" She growled. "They at least deserve to know that this is not my choice."

Giran's forehead wrinkled, and his eyes narrowed. "What do you mean, 'this isn't your choice'?"

Adan moved toward Cora to bite her hind leg yet again. Giran saw the movement and growled a menacing threat. The sound temporarily stunned Adan before he bit and bit hard. Cora jumped but not in the direction Adan had prompted. She faced her attacker in defiance as red liquid bubbled out of her fresh wound. "I'm not coming with you, Adan—not now—no matter how many threats you give."

Giran turned his intense stare from Adan to Cora. "What do you mean?"

"He's been threatening me for weeks. This morning, he said if I didn't come with him, he'd kill Sophia. His claw was on her neck as she lay sleeping. I didn't think it was a good time to argue with him, so I came. He's threatened Sophia before and Father. All to get me to be his mate."

Adan had been leaning back on his haunches as had Giran. Both were poised to strike at any moment. Adan kept his eyes on Giran but said to Cora. "Don't worry, Princess, when I'm done with you, I'll visit Sophia again. I don't want her to feel left out. I have just the right jaguar in mind for her."

The "Princess" issued a guttural hiss with twice the punch of a black howler and five times the venom of a golden frog. She leaped at Adan even though he was almost twice her size. Cora was small-framed, and beside Adan, she looked no bigger than a dwarfed jaguarundi. However, no one would have bet against her at that moment. She tore into Adan with a ferocity that only offended females can muster.

Giran looked to help, to intervene, but the path was so narrow. He kept getting pushed to the side by their twisting bodies and was afraid of biting Cora instead of Adan.

Size eventually trumped passion. Cora was pinned—her jugular exposed. Giran saw his opportunity and leaped into the fray. His shoulder connected with Adan's right flank and butted him off Cora and onto his side. Giran jumped over Cora and searched for any vulnerable piece of Adan flesh. The older and bigger jaguar quickly rolled back to all paws and lunged for Giran's leg. His jaw ripped into Giran's recent wound. Giran couldn't hold in the yelp of pain. His mind screamed for control. He knew his brother would attack again, and this time it would be fatal if he didn't regain focus.

The path around him became fuzzy like walking around in a low-hanging cloud. He sensed rather than saw two jaguars leap from behind and slam into Adan. His brother was again quick to his feet, but this time he retreated in lieu of Cora's cousins snarling between him and his quarry. Adan kept his head down with his tail tickling his belly in a show of submission. The tension was thicker than creek mud as the large jaguar backed away from a fight that would mean certain death for him.

After a few paces, Adan's demeanor changed from defeat to one of rebellion. "Watch out, little brother. We'll meet again real soon. Same goes for you—Cora dear."

With that, Cora's cousins charged, but Adan was already racing down the path. The two would give chase for some time—in vain. They'd never catch his brother.

The path was quiet now except for Cora's heavy panting. The blood from Adan's bite still oozed down her leg. Giran knelt to lick it away, not caring if it seemed forward or not. Turning to rest her head against Giran's shoulder, Cora let out a tiny cry. "Don't leave me, Giran. Please don't leave me."

He nudged her to look at him. Her brown eyes shimmered, and in the daytime, he could see sparkles of green emeralds shining like stars in the night sky. Giran felt her vulnerability, felt her fear, felt even the stirrings of her love.

"I won't leave you, Cora. I promise."

She nestled against him again and shook with sniffles and sobs. He stood strong, supporting her weight even though his leg was on fire. He spoke over and over again the soft words she wanted to hear, and the words he wanted to say. "Don't cry. I'm here, Cora. I won't leave you. I'm here."

Discussion Questions

1. Hasty-made promises are often regretted. What does God's word say about us keeping our promises? Numbers 30:2 says, "When a man makes a vow to the Lord or takes an oath to obligate himself by a pledge, he must not break his word but must do everything he said." (NIV)

2. What are some of God's promises, and how can we be assured that He will always be faithful to keep His word?

Chapter

13

The Pursuit of Justice

T he elders bent their necks toward the hive as far as they dared while Rhett pointed to the massive amounts of purple grains littering the fallen combs. "Look, there's the pollen from the Devil's Snare."

Elder Horado stepped back, his intense black stare commanding Rhett's attention. "Rhett, I don't understand what that purple dust has to do with anything."

"Elder, don't you see? This wasn't an accident. Someone knew what they were doing. Someone who knew that Devil's Snare pollen would quiet the bees. Not many creatures know that; it's mainly the prophets who pass along herbal knowledge. Most kinkajous—and kinkajous love honey—don't even know the secret of the Devil's Snare. They usually just grab a comb and run—stealing a few bites before the stings get too painful."

"So, what are you saying?" Elder Horado asked, head tilted. "Someone had it out for Tomás?"

"I don't know, Elder." Rhett thumped his tail on the sand and scratched his ear. "But I bet that same someone is responsible for the missing achiote."

The graying deer breathed in deeply and looked over his shoulder at the jungle wood. "Prophet," he said carefully, "I need to go find Tomás' parents."

Rhett stared at the departing marsh deer, frustration building in his chest. The elder either didn't believe him or didn't understand. Rhett paced the marshland where Tomás rested, one eye trained on the hovering vultures. The skunks and other onlookers had gone back to the mundane, leaving Rhett alone to ponder the happenings.

He needed a friend to bounce ideas off of. His mouth turned up slightly thinking about Giran. *He'd give me advice, whether I wanted it or not.* But there was no telling when the jaguar would return. His mom would listen, but he was trying not to draw her into all his prophet problems. If Mara were here, he might be brave enough to mention it to her, but she was off escorting another batch of orphans to Placero.

Rhett watched as the rising sun sprinkled orange diamonds on the dew-drenched marsh grass. Mesmerized, Rhett ceased his speculations. Like the rushing of fresh water over the highland cliffs, the moment of peace brought clarity. *Fattima did this!* Who knows where the snake picked up her knowledge of herbs? But she must have heard it somewhere and was sly enough to put it to use. But why? What does she have to gain from Tomás' death?

The questions continued to nibble his brain. He had to talk to her, had to stop her before another innocent got hurt.

✳✳✳

Rhett looked out on the temple courtyard from the top of one of the stone sentry figures guarding the entrance back into the jungle wild. This location in the southwestern corner of Sanchia was a better start site than the centrally located Wimba.

With Tirgato gone, the dilapidated human temple held no threat besides the Harpy eagle, and she was wary of crowds anyway. The eagle knew what was up though, listening from the top of her spiral perch. *Maybe she'd join us on the hunt?* Rhett snorted. *Imagine that—a Harpy as Sanchia's most cooperative citizen.*

Rhett turned his attention back to the courtyard. "No monkeys – again," Rhett grouched with a furrowed brow. He had meant to speak with Elder Mateo about missing the last Council, but it had slipped his mind after the bee incident.

Of course, this really wasn't a Council, but the messenger birds had made it clear that the elders, and additional able-bodied representatives from each family, were expected to be in attendance. The kinkajou elder wasn't even here and, while not terribly outspoken, at least Elder Oalo was usually faithful.

Where there should have been hundreds of creatures gathered, the courtyard instead looked barren, the open spaces filled with nothing but clouds of dust. The effects of the drought could be best seen away from the creeks on higher ground—like the temple mount. If there had been more rain, the courtyard, which had gone untended since Giran had left, would have been overtaken by all varieties of green fledglings. As it was, only a few of the heartier weeds showed their heads.

The animals stirred restlessly. Rhett couldn't wait any longer. He looked back down the path that led into the jungle in hopes of seeing a horde of latecomers. Empty.

Rhett cleared his throat. The eyes of those gathered turned his way. He felt the stares of deer, sloths, beavers, even several caimans that had traveled quite the distance on land. But the glaring lack of monkeys, lack of animals in general, was disheartening.

"Sanchian citizens." Rhett stood a little taller, hoping he looked more confident than he felt. "Since this is not a scheduled Council, we will not adhere to the usual formalities. However, I would like to begin by expressing my gratitude for your willingness to secure the safety of Sanchia."

Rhett paused to make sure his words had been absorbed. Then he continued. "As I am sure you have heard on the jungle vine, I believe Fattima is responsible for both the raid on the orphan's food supply as well as a premeditated attack on Tomás. However, she has not been found guilty yet, so please allow for questioning prior to justice. We will begin here and fan out across Sanchia, following the waterways. If she is spotted, please alert the nearest messenger bird who will then spread the word."

At this, Rhett had to pause because of the eruption of the flutter of wings. He couldn't help but smile at the show of support from his loyal followers. The flapping boosted the morale of the others gathered. *This might turn out okay, after all.*

"Prophet?" a voice called from the outskirts of the crowd. "I don't understand why snake hunting is the priority here lately. No one knows for sure if she's responsible for any of this business."

The beavers parted and showed some capybaras that must have shown up late along with a group of monkeys now watching from the wall. All eyes jerked from the elder capybara who had spoken back to Rhett. Rhett breathed deep, trying to form the right words but ended up in a coughing fit from a whirl of dust that had floated near.

By the time he could speak again, several of the animals had grouped and were whispering among themselves. He spoke as convincingly as he could. "Fattima is not guilty yet, but there are several reasons she is a suspect in Tomás' death and for the confiscated supplies."

With this, he cast a narrowed-eye glance at the monkeys on the wall who shuffled into the shadows.

"I just want to question her right now. If she is guilty, we'll hold the court proceedings."

One of the otters stepped forward. "My apologies, Prophet, but if Fattima doesn't want to be found, she's not going to be found. I know these waterways in and out. I just don't think it's possible if she's intent on hiding."

Elder Togro flew beside Rhett. "Hmph, speak for yourself, otter. We hawks can spot her two palm trees up."

The otters beat their tails on the dirt, stirring up a cyclone of choke hazards.

"Look, Sanchians." Rhett spoke with a paw outstretched for silence. "I understand this will be difficult. It would have been easier with more animals. But we will do the best we can to find Fattima and question her regarding the suspicious occurrences."

"Prophet, prophet," called a cotinga, flying into the middle of the startled assembly. "Trouble at Wimba. Trouble at home."

Rhett shook his head in frustration and turned to find Azul. The older bird would get the info out of this small cotinga better than him. "What sorta trouble, Azul? Can it wait?"

Azul conferred with the small yellow messenger and then reported, "Kinkajous have gathered. Dex is in trouble."

"Dex?" Rhett questioned, not expecting a reply. Dex was young, only a season older than his little brother. He might still be in the nursery section. "Naw," he mumbled. "He graduated last season."

"Azul, surely this isn't important enough that it can't wait until we're done here or better yet, have Elder Oalo take care of it?"

The bright blue bird shook her head slowly. "They've already beat him—will beat him more if you don't come."

Rhett's tail bristled. "Beat him. Why? What'd he do?" Rhett exclaimed.

"Dex stole."

Rhett inhaled sharply through his nostrils but then realizing what had to be done, hung his head in defeat. The hunt would have to go on without him. Stealing in the jungle was not a fluffy offense. Matters such as these, especially in a food shortage, could blossom and multiply faster than mosquitos after the rainy season.

"Elder Brayan, will you please organize and continue this hunt without me? I'll try to take care of this business and join back with you."

Nodding his head in unexcited acceptance, the elder otter said, "We'll do our best, Prophet, but no guarantees."

Rhett grunted and turned from the group to swing toward the Wimba. *No guarantees for sure. Half the group doesn't think she can be found, including Brayan, and the other half doesn't think she should be found.* Rhett knew exactly how far this hunt would go—about the distance of a gnat's nose. He'd have to find Fattima himself. But first, he'd have to deal with one of his own. "Little Dex? Stealing?" he huffed as he swung at a reckless speed back to the Wimba.

Discussion Questions

1. Why should justice only be administered by the government or appropriate legal system?

2. Consider the commandment, "Thou shalt not steal." What consequences come from this sin, and why is it harmful to yourself and others?

Chapter

14

Sanctuary Island

ora's sister, Sofia, had said his name was Sam, but Giran had trouble believing her. Why would a Prophet go by such a plain name? Now that Giran sat in the brush, hiding among the greenery beside a fast-flowing stream, he could see why. The illustrious anteater had his head half-buried in a dead log that must have floated onto his island beach. When not taken up by the business of swallowing, his light brown paws, the color of honey, scraped at the rotting wood. The fierce clawing caused his fleshy abdomen to jiggle like a marsh creek mud puddle.

Altura's Sanctuary was different from Sanchia's but had the same basic elements. The island provided the seclusion a Prophet needed, and the beaches around the stream were ample size to hold a Council. The island itself was roughly two palm trees wide and maybe twice as long. It sported a few scraggly trees alongside a towering Guanandi tree that rose above and sheltered the others like a mother among cubs. The entire island didn't appear sandy at all except for a thin ribbon barrier that separated the land from gently lapping waves.

Besides the Guanandi and its few minions, only brush grass and flowering Lobster Claws covered Sanctuary Island. The Lobster

Claws were the Kapoks of flowers. Most of the red and yellow blossoms stood taller than the Prophet himself. Giran cocked his head. A constant hum came from the island – the drone of a billion beetles swarming their favorite flower. *Aww. That's the reason behind the flowers: they attract easy meals for the Prophet.*

"You might as well swim over, Jaguar." A scratchy voice pulled Giran from his perusal of the island. "Or are you planning on becoming a permanent fixture of my stream-side view?" The anteater raised on hind legs, and his beady eyes stared directly at Giran.

Giran didn't speak, didn't move. *How does he know I'm here? Surely he can't see me with his ant eyes.*

"Well?" the Prophet asked, his tone impatient. "Night is coming, and I'd prefer to finish my dinner in peace. Leave or swim—do something."

Giran had come to talk to the Prophet, but now, his brain was pond scum. He couldn't think of why he wanted to see the strange creature. *Hopefully, I'll remember before I get over to his island, or I won't be able to stay in Altura whether I want to or not. I'll be banished for stupidity. Wait, that's it. I need to know what the Sovereign thinks about me staying here.*

With renewed mission, Giran stepped out of the tangle of grasses and palm roots. His back leg caught on an errant vine, and at the last second—he face-planted into the mud. "This is not going well," he murmured and shook his leg to free it from the villainous vine. Unfettered at last, he padded into the stream and swam toward the island.

When his legs felt the sand rise up under-paw, he walked onto the Prophet's home and shook dry. Unfortunately, the Prophet happened to be within spraying distance.

"Please, really!" Sam spat in disgust. "Do you have to do that so…so thoroughly? A little water never hurt anyone."

Giran looked up sheepishly. "Sorry, Prophet. I didn't think." It was then that he noticed two things about Sam the Prophet. First— the eyes. Up close they reminded him of Rhett's, but he couldn't for the life of him explain why. Looking in them was like staring into a dark, bottomless pool—the kind of pool cubs are warned to avoid. Second, he had a triangle marking on his head. His was different from Rhett's and different from Saloma's too if Giran remembered right. Sam sported a three-sided patch of cloud-white fur on a snout painted tan. But a triangle it was—the unmistakable marking of a rainforest Prophet.

The Prophet cocked his narrow head. "I don't remember you but, of course, there are too many jaguars in Altura to keep up. Your accent says you're in Vinícius' clan." An intense stare from the Prophet held Giran's attention. "Or … are you recently from Sanchia?"

The young jaguar nodded his head. "I'm staying as a guest of Elder Ramiro."

"Interesting. Why wouldn't you stay with those who migrated from Sanchia, or didn't you know they were here?"

"I didn't intend on staying here at all. I was wounded by man's fire stick, and Ramiro's clan took me in."

"Oh, that's interesting indeed. I assume you're recovering?"

"Yes, Prophet, I am."

"Then why are you here if you don't need medical help? That's the only reason the jaguars have ever come to me, and that hasn't happened in seasons."

Giran cocked his head to study the Prophet. Sam turned away from Giran's stare with a shrug before adding, "They feel no need for a Prophet. None of the animals do."

"What about the feud between the jaguars—the raids, the bad blood? Don't you care?"

"I might could've helped them at the beginning—if they had wanted my advice, which they didn't. Now, it's too late. Besides, they'll work it out themselves or kill each other in the process."

"What do you do then?" Giran blurted.

"Do?" Sam chuckled. "I tend my Lobster buds, enjoy my meals, and relish the peace and quiet."

Giran pawed at the marsh grass until specks of white sand dotted the green. "But I need help," he whispered.

"I thought you said you were healing just fine?"

"I am. I need a different kind of help, from someone who knows the Sovereign. I want to know the right thing to do and how to do it."

The Prophet looked out on the stream flowing around them. When he spoke, his tone was wistful, longing. "The Sovereign isn't here anymore. He left a long time ago. I haven't heard or dreamed or felt anything in many, many seasons."

Giran stared at him with his mouth hanging open. "How'd that happen?"

Sam turned his eyes away. "I'm not really sure. It was a slow happening that didn't seem important at the time. The animals started answering their own questions and solving their own problems. They came to Councils less and less until it was just me and the birds."

The Prophet turned a sharp eye to Giran. "Why do you care, anyway? What do you want—a word from the Sovereign? Good luck with that."

Giran thought it best not to reply and instead backed into the water. "This isn't the place for answers," he mumbled, though louder than he meant to.

Prophet Sam dropped back to all fours and dug at his log again. "I'm sorry you're disappointed. Truth be known, I am too."

Giran let the stream pull him in and away from Sanctuary Island, on into the heart of Altura. The cool water comforted him as he strove to understand the conversation he had just had. *Could this happen to Rhett? To Sanchia?* He wasn't sure, but he felt the need to at least warn Rhett about the situation here in Altura.

The urgency collided with his heart's desire for Cora and family. That was why he had come in the first place – to find jaguars. He needed a solution, a way to stay here, and a way to go back. Both, he needed to do both. But how? Nothing made sense anymore. The

Prophet was supposed to help him—tell him what the Sovereign expected.

Giran floated along amidst the orange sparkles of a setting sun with no thought as to the passing of time. He drifted until the stream branched and then swam to shore on a dark, forgotten beachhead. He had never felt so alone.

Discussion Questions

1. What is the problem with Sam giving up the leadership position that he was appointed by the Sovereign to hold? What are the consequences for those living in Altura?

2. Giran said, "This isn't the place for answers." Was he right? Where should we look for answers when we need to make an important decision?

3. Sometimes we drift from where God wants us slowly, and before we know it, we feel far away from our Heavenly Father. What are some things we can do to make sure that doesn't happen in our spiritual life?

Chapter

15

Quick Tempered Judgment

Rhett's kinsmen crowded around the foot of the Wimba. He could hear their angry cries as he ran across the open field. A few tapirs and monkeys milled about as well. *Why are they here and not at the hunt?*

At first, the group didn't notice Rhett's arrival. They were too focused on Dex, or quarreling, or both. The Prophet skirted the crowd from the back and scrambled up the Wimba. From the platform, he spotted the huddled kinkajou, surrounded by a sea of angry faces.

Upon noticing his presence, the monkeys moved to the back and danced from leg to leg in anticipation of the show to come. The tapirs turned their nose up at him with their usual haughty look. Rhett wiped a bead of sweat from his face that had nothing to do with his recent sprint across the field. "I wish they weren't here," he muttered. "They always show up when there's a kinkajou issue. I wonder if Saloma had to deal with that when there was a sloth disagreement.

86

Do they really think I'll treat my own better than the others?" Rhett twisted his paws in frustration.

"What's going on, Elder Oalo?" Rhett asked the aged kinkajou standing over Dex. His face looked longer than usual—his fur grayer. He had a few bright red scratches on him as well. *Who's the elder been scrapping with?*

Elder Oalo sighed and relaxed his stance when he heard Rhett's authoritative tone. "Prophet, Dex here stole a mango from the nursery stock."

"How do you know it was him? Someone see him?"

Looking down at Dex, Elder Oalo shook his head and sighed. "Dex was seen hiding in the shadows during full sun, eating a mango. At sunset, the nursery workers counted the mangoes along with the other fruits and came up one short. They keep close tabs on them these days."

Rhett considered this and asked the group. "Who saw him eating the mango?"

Two kinkajous, Buck and Roald, raised their paws. Rhett remembered them from his younger days, as they were about his age. They were brothers—always together—which was a good thing. They weren't the brightest stars in the kinkajou family, but between the two of them, they made do. *Which one should I address?* Rhett wondered before deciding on both.

"Buck, Roald, what exactly did you see? But first, why were you out in full sun anyway?"

Both answered. "We waz…" They startled each other by speaking at the same time and stopped to stare at one another.

Rhett rolled his eyes. "Roald, what happened?"

"Well Rhett …"

Azul squawked, batting at the Wimba branches with his wings to draw the attention of the crowd. "Prophet! His title is Prophet!"

Roald, wide-eyed, stared at Azul and then at Elder Oalo. Then he squeaked out, "I'm ssssorry, Rhett. And then quickly corrected, "I mean … I'm sorry, Prophet."

Rhett swallowed hard and looked down at his paws—stiff and sore from stress rubbing.

"That's okay, Roald. Just, what happened?"

"Well, we waz going to bed. Late cause we waz playing scrib-scratch, and I waz winning."

"No, you ..." started Buck.

"Buck," Elder Oalo said, silencing the kinkajou with his deep tone.

Roald puffed his chest and continued. "I waz winning, and then we heard a branch snap. We looked and saw Dex swinging by. We followed him. Almost lost him when he stopped swinging, but then we saw him crawling under a sage bush. We smelled it then—the ripe mango. Crawled close and caught him red-pawed, cramming his face with it."

Rhett wanted to pause to take in all he had heard, but the insistent stares of the kinkajous, tapirs, and monkeys demanded action. "Buck, is this what happened?"

Buck nodded his head but kept silent.

"Afterwards, Roald. What'd you do?"

"We drug him out. We knew he'd stolen it. Where else would he have gotten a mango?"

Rhett had a feeling that more than just a polite interchange occurred as was confirmed by a closer look at Dex's swelling jaw.

"And then?" Rhett questioned, looking hard at Roald.

"Then Elder Oalo came along. He had us wait until after the nursery count, then brought us all here." Roald fidgeted with the dirt while he spoke.

Rhett didn't bother asking how Elder Oalo just happened along—it wasn't important anyway. But it did explain the elder's scratches. The old kinkajou must have had a heap of trouble stopping the brawl.

"Dex," Rhett said. The hunched kinkajou barely raised his head. "Did you steal a mango from the nursery stock?" Rhett's spine tightened in fierce hope that the youth had been falsely accused.

Stealing in ordinary times was a major infraction; stealing in drought and famine was almost capital.

"Yes, Prophet," Dex answered in a small voice.

Rhett slumped. Not the answer he had hoped for. He didn't need to ask, "why." He knew why. All the gatherers were crazy for fruit of any kind. But Dex wasn't starving yet. He had termites to eat just like Rhett, Roald, and Buck.

The tapirs mumbled and pawed at the dry grass with their hooves. The monkeys jabbered with a few rather loud jeers of "rat thief." Rhett narrowed his eyes. *Why aren't they trying to find Fattima? They could be doing something useful rather than taunting small kinkajous.*

"Monkeys, tapirs," he called, "this is a kinkajou issue. Why are you even here? You should be on the hunt."

One of the larger and older monkeys hollered from the back. "We're here because it is a kinkajou issue. How do we know you won't excuse your kin when they break the law?"

Rhett's mouth dropped. No adequate words could combat that level of disrespect.

Another monkey added. "The hunt for Fattima is pointless. You don't have any evidence against her. Why should we waste our energy tracking down a snake just because she offended you? Naw, I'm not wasting my time!"

"Yeah." The tapirs joined in the protest. "How does a snake hunt help the food shortage?"

Rhett clenched his fists. *What right do they have to question my judgments? Saloma didn't have to deal with this.* He looked at the faces staring back at him, waiting for an answer. The tapirs looked hardened; the monkeys had a mocking grin. Rhett couldn't tell what the kinkajous were thinking; he never could understand his own kind.

Rhett stood a little taller on the overhanging Wimba branch. "I am here to ensure justice, and that includes both Dex and Fattima. She will have her chance to answer to her crimes, as Dex will answer for his."

Several of the monkeys rolled their eyes. Rhett's patience evaporated like a school of minnows before a piranha.

"Dex, pay back the mango three times or be banished to the wastelands at next full moon. The rest of you are in danger of rebellion and banishment yourselves if you don't join the hunt now!"

Fear replaced mockery, and animals scattered. Dex and Elder Oalo were the only two that stayed, staring up at him like prey before a crouching jaguar.

Rhett couldn't stand to meet their unbelieving eyes. *What have I done? Why did I answer so quickly?* Three to one is the standard for theft, but Dex won't find three mangoes—Dex won't find one. He'll die for sure.

"Rhett?" a familiar voice questioned quietly. He turned around.

"Mara?"

Discussion Questions

1. Rhett dispensed punishment in haste and in anger. Authority figures in our lives, such as parents or teachers, need at times to punish wrongdoing. What are some recommendations you would offer for the administering of fair yet merciful discipline?

Chapter

16

The Trap

"I shouldn't have floated so far." Giran grumbled as he made his way upstream. For all he knew, he might have sailed right out of Altura. He certainly had drifted deep into the lowlands; his legs told him that. As he steadily climbed uphill, trying to make it back to the caves, his muscles ached and screamed for relief. Every now and then he would cross the stream, partly because he needed to cool his burning leg muscles and partly for a change of scenery. Mostly though, he chose the easiest side for travel. In many sections, one side of the stream would open up into strands of smooth sand instead of long sections of tangled green vines that looked eager to devour any wanderer.

Unfortunately, the number of beaches decreased the further upstream he walked. Traveling through the thick brush took time and effort. Occasionally he would venturea way from the stream in hopes of a path or clearing, but Altura's jungle region was fiercely untamed. He could now understand a little better why the old Sanchian cats coveted Cora's caves.

"Everything is about Cora these days." He mumbled while spitting out some sweat that had trickled into his mouth. He pushed through an especially dense and clingy marsh brush to land back on a small beach head. *Why did I go and tell her I wouldn't leave? I have to leave her. I've gotta go home for Rhett's sake.*

These same questions had been swarming him for days like flies on a day-old carcass. "Sam wasn't any help," he whined. "If you can't ask a Prophet, who can you ask?"

Giran had been talking to himself ever since he floated away from the Prophet—not minding if someone overheard. He didn't know any of these creatures anyway, so why should he care if they knew his business? When he took a moment to catch his breath, he heard a faint cry—a jaguar's cry. Giran froze, one ear cocked to the clouds.

That was definitely a call for help. But this far into the lowlands, it must be one of the other jaguars, not Cora's family, not his family. Giran stood listening, swishing flies with his tail. *I might have heard wrong. Even if I did hear something, I shouldn't get involved, not in another tribe's business.*

The call sounded again—his time a bit weaker—and his conscience joined the conversation. *What if none of the others are near enough to hear?*

Giran reluctantly lowered his head and pushed through the underbrush toward the sound. He couldn't let a cry for help go unanswered—especially a jaguar's call.

The floor opened a few palm tree lengths from the stream to reveal a path—a well-trod trail littered with animal droppings. The path veered back the way Giran had come. He would most likely have intersected it had he kept traveling upstream. He stooped to sniff the broken grass causing the hairs on his neck to stiffen.

Man had been here recently; he was sure of it. He had smelled that artificial odor drifting on the wind from the barges on the Great River.

I don't want any part of man. He fretted, turning his head back and forth to spot the potential evil.

The cry of pain came again from the direction the path took as it veered toward the stream. Giran knew he must hurry. He wished he could travel along the outside of the path, carefully hidden by the brush, but the undergrowth in this part of the jungle was too thick, and the going would be too slow. He'd have to risk the open path. Decision made, he trotted ahead, ever vigilant for the source of the human scent.

When Giran first saw the jaguar, lying by the side of the road, he had no idea why the call for help. The large cat looked fine from the back. After a few more tail lengths, Giran figured it out. The jaguar was gnawing on the back of his left leg – a leg rooted to the ground by an iron vine.

"Giran? Is that you?" The jaguar had turned to face him.

Giran instinctively crouched on his hind legs, panicking. *Is this a trap? Will Adan attack? I can't defend myself against my brother. He made that clear a few days ago.*

"Giran? You going to leave me?" Adan asked in a gruff tone, nose twitching in the air.

"You'd leave me." The words popped out of Giran's mouth without any thought. If he had taken a second, he would have bitten back the words, no matter if it was the truth.

Adan turned his head back around to gnaw on his leg again. "Yeah, you're right. I would."

Giran didn't know what to do. If he freed his brother, Adan would continue to terrorize Cora and her family, not to mention himself. The open path to the side of Adan looked inviting, welcoming. If he closed his eyes and walked real fast, he would be away from the sight in a second. Soon, he wouldn't even be able to hear the cries for help.

He pawed at an errant root that crossed the path. *Why did I come in the first place? Now, how can I leave my own brother here to die in man's trap?*

Shaking his head as if to shake out the temptation to run, he strode over to stand above Adan. His brother's leg was encased in iron teeth. Out of desperation, Adan had been gnawing at the bone right above the jaws. Bright red blood oozed over the smooth surface of the man's trap. The white of his brother's bone shone like a full moon at midnight.

Giran knelt beside his brother and licked the wound, hoping to staunch the flow of blood. He could gnaw the leg off and free his brother, but both knew what would then happen to a handicapped jaguar. Still, that would be better than being captured by man.

Adan had been watching him inspect the wound. His brother's eyes were glossy, but his lips were pursed, daring Giran to think he had been crying. Giran sighed in sympathy, followed by Adan's sigh of defeat. The older jaguar bowed his head. "I know what it means. I knew the second it happened."

"Why, Adan, did you go near it? Didn't you smell the metal—the man?"

"I didn't smell anything but pork, Giran." He hung his head even lower. "It's always been a weakness of mine, and the trap was covered by a flank of pork fat."

Giran looked at the trap. There was no sign of pork fat left, which wasn't surprising.

"Go on, Giran." Adan said. "Do what you have to do, and I'll be grateful."

The evil device was two pieces. One looked like a metal jaw with shiny gray teeth that fastened around Adan's leg like a Harpy's claws around a rabbit's throat, relentless and uncompromising. Coming off the metal jaw was a man-made vine that snaked into the brush. Giran tugged on it and saw it was rooted to a nearby tree. *Maybe I can knock down the tree? That'd free him.* Then the second thought caught up with him: *free him to walk around the rest of his life with a metal vine following him. That'd make for good hunting.*

Giran suddenly perked up. "Adan, I'll go get the Prophet. He'll know what to do."

Adan looked at him like he would look at a monkey who had sniffed too many ripe mangoes. "Sam, that long-nosed rodent? He doesn't know anything. Maybe Saloma would have—but Sam?"

"Someone would have trained Sam a long time ago. Surely Altura had a Prophet before him? Maybe that Prophet taught him something." Giran waited while Adan soaked up the suggestion. "What could it hurt? Before we, you know …"

Adan shrugged. "I guess it won't hurt to ask. But what if the man returns before you come back?" Then his eyes narrowed. "Or will you come back?"

Giran rolled his own eyes. "I wouldn't make the suggestion if I was planning to run away."

"Fine." Adan huffed with a smirky grin. "But hurry up. I'm dying here."

Giran cocked his head to study and yes, even slightly admire, his older half-brother. In as gruesome of a situation as this was, who but Adan could keep a sense of humor?

Discussion Questions

1. Read Luke 10:25-37. How does the story above relate to the story told by Jesus?

2. Have you ever been in a situation where you needed to show kindness to someone who had wronged you? How did you respond, and how could you have possibly handled it better?

Chapter

17

Family Conference

"I know snakes can climb trees, Rhett. That's not the point!" Brianna, paws on hip, gave no illusions of submission to the Prophet – not today—not in her nook. The harsh sunrays were trying their best to invade the small cracks in the canopy above, just like Rhett was trying to budge the solid rock of his mother. The thought of Fattima threatening and holding them captive like Tirgato had done set his tail to quivering.

"What is the point then, Mom? What would it hurt for you to move to the Wimba? I don't want you in danger again because of me."

"Rhett, I have my own life to live. The twins are doing well in school. I'm not about to pick up and move into that tree in the middle of nowhere."

Rhett picked up his tail to fidget. *Tail-wringing is becoming a bad habit.* The image of his beautiful tail, hairless and pink, flashed through his mind. He flung it out of reach. This conversation wouldn't even be happening if the hunt had been successful. But all the teams, such as they were, reported back with no sign of Fattima.

Brianna put a paw on Rhett's shoulder. "Listen, Fattima would have great difficulty even crawling to the base of our tree, much less all the way up to our platform. She's the size of three river dolphins. Even if she made it up here, she couldn't reach us in our nooks. I just don't see the big threat."

Rhett sighed. He couldn't argue with his mom, never could. "How about I station a caracara here, just for a while until things clear up? They could sound the warning if something should go wrong."

"Fine, Rhett. Just make sure it sets up nest down-tree from us. I don't want to be scrubbing their splattering off my clean platform."

The side of Rhett's mouth twitched. Briana was a perfectionist when it came to her spotless floor. Over the seasons, he had endured countless scoldings regarding her prim platform.

Brianna must have taken his smile as acquiescence and moved to sit against the strangler vine that served as the main entry tunnel and one of the three supporting pillars of their nest. "So, Mara stopped by here yesterday."

At the mention of Mara's name, Rhett eyed the exit that Brianna now blocked. *What uncomfortable and potentially embarrassing conversation does she have in mind?*

Brianna looked back at him with a smug grin that soon faded back into seriousness. "Did Mara tell you that the neighboring regions are closed to orphans now? We've exhausted our welcome."

Rhett sat beside his mom, stretching his legs and tail across the braided decking. "I was afraid of that this time. We sent a lot. Did she say if all found homes?"

"Yeah, but it took her a while, and she had to double back to Cantiga and Placero. They were the most accommodating, but even so, they made it clear that they didn't have the means to support any more."

"I don't know what else to do, Mom," Rhett said in a high-pitched tone. "If the drought and famine weren't bad enough, Fattima is plotting against everything I try."

Brianna put her paw on his. "Have you asked the Sovereign?"

Rhett huffed without thinking and then regretted it after seeing Brianna's wilted countenance. "The Sovereign doesn't answer. I don't know what to think. All I have are strange dreams about fire."

Brianna drew her forehead fur together like a brown mohawk. "Fire? Why fire? What does that mean?"

Rhett swallowed a sarcastic and most likely disrespectful comment.

Brianna smirked. "Sorry. You caught me off guard. I know you can't be expected to understand everything yet. Fire is strange, but the Sovereign has sent strange dreams before. Remember Saloma talking about some of her old dreams?"

Rhett nodded. "Yeah, I remember. But it doesn't make sense— even if it means something. What does fire have to do with helping with a famine? A fire would be the death blow to Sanchia."

Both sat tense, shuddering at the thought of what fire would do to their jungle home. Brianna spoke first. "Rhett, I don't understand either, but I know the Sovereign hasn't forgotten you. He is doing something—I'm sure of it."

"But Mom, why is He so silent when we need Him?"

Brianna said nothing for a while but then squeezed Rhett's paw. "It's going to be okay, Rhett. You'll see. The Sovereign hasn't abandoned you. You'll see."

Rhett looked over at his mom and squeezed her paw back. He wouldn't argue the point—he hoped she was right.

"Did Mara tell you anything at all about the trip?" Brianna asked.

"Not much," Rhett said quietly. After an awkward silence, he added, "I was busy when she stopped by."

"Busy?" she asked with a raised eye. She'd seen the statement for the rotten mush it was. "Mara's been gone for almost a whole moon. Why didn't you two go hang out somewhere?"

Rhett squirmed a little farther away from Brianna. He did not want to have this conversation. "I don't know, Mom. We talked ... some. She mentioned to me Placero's temporary cat idea, and I agreed it was a bad one. Hiring cats to wreak overnight terror on the gatherers would bring trauma – not balance."

"So that's all you two talked about when you haven't seen each other in a whole moon?"

Rhett stood and walked to the edge of the platform. A slight breeze ruffled his fur. "Maybe it'll rain—it feels like rain," he said, hoping to throw off the impending conversation.

"What's wrong, Rhett? You must know that she's expecting you to ask her to covenant. She's waiting."

"She said that?" Rhett turned sharply toward his mother.

"She didn't have to. You know she's not like the other kinkajous, neither are you. A covenant is the Sovereign's way to start a family, and she wants a covenant—believes you want one too."

Rhett turned back to stare at the shadows waltzing along the jungle floor below. "I want one, with her too. It's just …"

"Just what? You two together are perfect."

"She's well, she's perfect, but I'm not. I don't want her to be disappointed. If I can get better at this Prophet job, then maybe I'll be …. be good enough."

Brianna walked out to the edge and put her paw on Rhett's shoulder. "She's not looking for perfect, Rhett. That's your expectation, not hers."

Rhett huffed and shook his head. "It's …it's well, Dad too."

Brianna stepped back. "Your dad? What does he have to do with it?"

Rhett saw comprehension dawn in her eyes along with the hurt that rolled with it.

"Mom, I know Dad's a good kinkajou. I love seeing him when he comes, but Mara might not understand."

Brianna put her paws on her hips for the second time that morning. "You're right—he is a good kinkajou."

Rhett hung his head. "I'm sorry, Mom. I'm not ashamed of Dad being a pet—but you know what others would say—how they would treat you and the twins if they knew."

"Others' is not Mara, Rhett. I think you're selling her short. If she cares about you and me, then she's not going to go squirrelly when she meets your dad."

As a cub, he had thought his father had the best job in the jungle, sailing the big river. Then he began to understand the teasing jokes about pets and realized just who his dad was – what his dad was. He wasn't free; he belonged to a man.

The image of his dad on his trading boat came to mind. He could see him swinging from the masts and scampering across the wooden boxes of goods. "Wooden boxes of goods!" He murmured out loud.

"What'd you say?" Brianna looked at him with head cocked.

"Boxes and boxes of food. That's it!"

Discussion Questions

1. How do we know that God hears our prayers even if sometimes we feel He's either not listening or not answering?

2. To what extent should we be concerned about what other people think?

Chapter

18

Freedom

The Prophet wasn't on his beach when Giran swam to shore. It seemed rude to shout and rude to snoop. Fortunately, he didn't have to shuffle on the sand for long.

"Back so soon with more questions?" came an inquiry from above, sarcasm dripping like drool off a hungry dog.

The brown tuft of hair on the anteater's neck bristled as he climbed down the massive Guanandi tree. Compassion softened the harsh replies Giran may have been tempted to throw back. *He's prepared for a snide comment—anticipating ridicule.*

Instead of giving the expected, Giran answered, "I apologize for disturbing your rest, Prophet. My brother is caught in man's trap. We need your help."

"Help!" the anteater spit. "I don't know how to help anyone. You've come to the wrong place...again." Prophet Sam turned to crawl back up the Guanandi.

"No, wait, Prophet."

Sam stopped and turned his snout back in Giran's direction but didn't show any commitment.

"Look, it's a metal jaw with teeth that grips on both sides and an iron vine rooted to the base of a tree. Have you seen one?"

The Prophet took a moment. "Yeah, I've seen them," he said dryly.

"Well, do you know how to get it off?"

The anteater gazed skyward toward his nest with a longing akin to a cat stalking a juicy peccary. Giran huffed. The sun would be up soon, and man came out with the sun. His patience with the Prophet was waning. After what seemed to Giran like moons, Sam finally answered, "I've never released one, not by myself. It takes two creatures."

Hope rose in Giran's chest. "Well, me – you, we have two."

The anteater shook his head, tapping his long snout on the trunk. Frustration or coincidence, Giran wasn't sure. "You don't understand. The last time I even helped was with my teacher, so many seasons ago I almost forgot it even happened."

"You'll remember, I'm sure you will. Come and see."

The Prophet squinted his eyes and peered down his nose at Giran. "Who are you?"

"I'm nobody, just a jaguar with a hurt brother. Please come and help."

The Prophet sighed in defeat.

It didn't take long for them to float downriver, but forever for Giran to fight through the brush along the stream, making a way for himself and Sam. Giran heaved a sigh of relief when they reached the path, now well-lit by the morning sun. They trotted a few palm tree lengths up the trail until Adan came into view.

"You're back," Adan said through gritted teeth. He didn't sit up this time. Giran wondered if he would have the strength to survive even if they did manage to remove the metal jaw.

"Oh, and you've brought Prophet Sam."

At least he used his title, even if it did sound borderline saucy.

Sam walked over to Adan and bent to study the trap.

"So, Sam. You know what to do, or shall we all commence with chewing?"

Giran shook his head. *So much for respect for the Prophet.*

The Prophet didn't acknowledge Adan's question. In fact, he turned away from Adan and crawled into the heavy brush beside the path. When the greenery closed in behind the anteater, Giran and Adan just looked at each other in disbelief.

"Well, that was helpful." Adan sneered.

"You could've been nicer." Giran retorted back, a little annoyed at his brother's attitude after all the work he had put in to get the Prophet.

Sam poked his snout out of the brush, surprising them both. "Are you coming?" he grunted with impatience.

Giran ventured a confused look at Adan before plunging into the brush behind the anteater.

"Over here," Sam called.

"He can really move through this brush," Giran mumbled, trying to push through the clinging vines. *I guess I didn't need to clear a path for him earlier.* When he emerged back into the open, the anteater was gnawing on a low branch a few paw lengths off the ground.

"Here, bite this branch into two pieces." The Prophet pushed on the weakened side with his surprisingly useful, all-purpose snout.

Following a cracking sound, a sturdy branch the width of Giran's tail landed in front of him. He assumed the Prophet meant for him to chew two fairly equal-sized pieces, so he eyed the wood and dug in. By the time he had separated the branch into two sticks, the Prophet was by his side, ready to bite one. "Come on," he grunted, charging back into the brush.

Dragging a stick in his mouth while burrowing through the brush was way harder than before, and it irked that he couldn't keep up with the anteater. By the time Giran stepped back out onto the path, the Prophet stood by the trap, again studying it with his tiny black eyes.

"I think I remember what to do." The Prophet leaned back on his two back legs.

"You think?" asked Adan in a small voice. He was getting weaker.

"Here Prophet." Giran dropped the stick and leaped to his side. "Tell me what to do. I'm sure you remember." Inside though, Giran had to shake away a few doubts. Sam hadn't exactly exhibited much Prophet potential.

The anteater nodded with his long snout. "Pick that stick back up. But before, let me show you what to do. I want you to point that stick like you're going to poke the trap. Then gently pry the end between the claw teeth until you hit the back flat portion of the trap. I'll do the same thing from the other side. Once we're in position, I'll blink twice, and you'll know I'm ready. Then push hard against your stick."

Prophet Sam stopped and looked at Adan. "Adan, for this to work, you must pull your leg out of the trap once you see it wide enough. I'm going to have my mouth full, so you'll have to watch and do it at the right time. Understand?"

Adan turned a nauseous shade of pale green. Giran wasn't sure at all if he could manage to stay conscious, let alone pull his leg out.

"Isn't there a way we can help him?" Giran asked the Prophet.

"That's what we're doing," Sam spit back. He paused, perhaps regretting his harsh tone, and added, "You're right. We really need one other creature. But I'm afraid it wouldn't be in his best interest to leave and go find one now. The sun is already full up – the man will return to his trap soon."

"Ok, then," Giran said with more confidence than he felt. "Let's get on with it. Adan, you ready?"

Adan didn't bother answering, other than a faint nod. Giran picked up his stick and moved opposite Sam. The first part, trying to maneuver the stick between the iron teeth and into position, was tricky. Adan, to his credit, didn't whimper, though he flinched a few times. Giran glanced over at him at one point, and his eyes were sealed shut. "He better open them soon, or he'll miss his opportunity." Giran swished him with his tail, and his brother stirred.

Once both sticks were pressed against opposite sides, he saw the blinks of the anteater. He pushed. Faster than a fly's flap, it was over. He heard the snap of the jaw come back together and saw Adan's leg lying beside him in a little puddle of crimson mud.

Giran started licking the wound but stopped when Prophet Sam nudged him with his snout. "You both need to get away from here first. Then, tend to his wounds. He'll need honey and a whole lot of rest if he wants to keep that leg."

The Prophet looked down at Adan. "I mean it. If you try to rush the healing, it'll get infected, and there's no Prophet in the Amazon who could help you then, much less me. Understand?"

Without another word, the Prophet scurried over to the brush and disappeared. *I didn't even say thank you,* Giran fretted. But chasing him now would be useless—helping Adan was more important.

"Well, brother. Let's get you well. If we're going to continue our feud, I want you healthy."

Adan looked hard at him. "Giran, why'd you help me? You know I wouldn't have done the same."

Giran bit his lower lip. He wasn't sure how to explain it. "I did it because it's what the Sovereign would want me to do. You might not know about the Sovereign, but my mom taught me lots of songs about him when I was a cub. Then Saloma and Rhett—they reminded me about Him. Well, I pledged to live my life for the Sovereign. He wouldn't want me to leave you here to die, so I didn't. Ya see?"

Adan shook his head. He didn't see. Giran sighed. *I knew I was going to mess that up.*

"Here, let's get you safe, and I'll tell you about it later." With that, Giran moved beside Adan and used all his weight to push against his brother, supporting him as the bigger jaguar stood on three legs. Adan winced with his first awkward step. As they hobbled away, Giran softly hummed one of the ancient melodies about the Sovereign. It was a shame he didn't remember but a few of the words. They might have brought comfort as well. After the song,

Giran heard the rustle of brush vines alongside the path. *So, Sam didn't leave us after all.*

Discussion Questions

1. Giran helped Adan because of his lifelong pledge to the Sovereign. Have you done something, maybe something you didn't necessarily want to do, because of your commitment to Christ?

Chapter

19

The Great Boat Heist

The Great River was as black as the panther's hide, with only a ribbon of moonlight weaving along the surface. The darkness would come in handy during the operation, but right now, it made it difficult to spot the boat. Added to the darkness, was the constant churning of the water, drowning out any sounds that would be made by the approaching craft. So Rhett sat, perfectly still, squinting up-river toward the bend. The birds he had stationed farther up had reported that a boat, heavily laden with boxes, was on its way.

"Is one near, Rhett?" whispered a voice from behind, almost startling him off his tree perch.

"Mara," he huffed. Her face fell. "I'm sorry, Mara. You startled me. What are you doing here? Who told you I'd be here?"

"Your mom. She's worried, Rhett. Me too. I came because I needed to talk to you."

"Now?" Rhett asked before turning his attention back up-river. "Now is not a good time to talk. Tomorrow maybe?"

"Rhett," Mara whispered. "I don't think this is a good idea."

Rhett kept his focus on the coming boat. "I'm sorry, Mara. I really will have some time after tonight. Then, we can talk all you want."

"You didn't hear what I said. I don't think what you're about to do is right."

Rhett turned then and looked into her eyes. Even in this situation, her eyes, her scent, her very presence shot tingles down his tail. *What did she say again?*

Mara rolled her eyes at his blank expression. "Dealing with man is never a good idea. We were taught that from birth, remember? Didn't Brianna and Saloma teach you that?"

"This is different, Mara. We have to. There's no other option. They have food—lots of it on those boats. The boxes you see from shore are filled with mangoes and nuts, bananas and acai." Just the thought of the delicacies made his mouth water. "Think about it, Mara, mangoes, tons of them. Dex won't have to be exiled. I can give him the three mangoes he needs."

"But it's stealing, Rhett. Even if it's to help Dex and the other animals—even if it is man—I don't think it's right to steal another creature's food. You're not acting any different than Dex."

Rhett scratched at his chin and sat up straight, taller than Mara. "The rules around stealing are rather debatable. Our law only deals with other creatures; it never mentions how to treat man. Anyway, where do you think they got the fruit, Mara? They stole it from our jungle. And do they ever pay?"

Mara shrugged. "You're at least right about that—man takes and never gives." She shook her head. "Even so—and I'm not saying I agree with that—but how are you planning on doing it without them hurting you with one of their sticks?"

The dreaded fire stick was a fear that plagued even a Prophet's sleep. Unlike the scary hyena stories from cub days, fire sticks were real – very real and dangerous.

Mara looked down at her paws, her face long. Rhett knew he should feel guilty about causing her to worry, but instead, the thought that she cared about him warmed him from the tips of his ears to the tip of his tail.

Rhett placed his paw on her shoulder. "Don't worry, Mara, I have a plan. See this stick?" he asked while revealing a branch tucked under his legs that was the size of an average monkey's tail. "I'm gonna use this to distract the guard at the wheel. Then I use this …"

Mara interrupted—her shiny eyes imploring. "You won't hurt the man, will you?"

"Of course not. It's just like Bong and Bash that we used to play as cubs, only his head is a bit bigger than a kinkajou's. He'll wake up with a headache, nothing more."

Mara didn't say anything, so he assumed she approved at least that part of the plan. "Like I was saying, Then, I use this …" and he drew her gaze to the vine wrapped around his waist, "to secure the door leading to the lower deck. The other men won't be able to come up to deck. You see, Mara, all safe."

Not just a brow, but Mara's whole side of her face lifted in a skeptical manner. "And how do you know so much about boats?"

Rhett turned his head back upriver so fast that it made him dizzy. "I just know."

"Well, that fills me with confidence." Mara retorted with biting sarcasm.

Rhett pursed his lips. *I'm not sure I like this side of Mara.*

"What about Bruno and Brutus over there? Why would you choose monkeys to help you; you know they can't be trusted? And Howler monkeys? They couldn't keep quiet if you promised them five boats of bananas."

"Elder Mateo assured me that these two could and would keep their mouths shut. I didn't want to use the monkeys, but they're the only ones strong enough to move the boxes. Can you imagine how many kinkajous it would take to move those crates? Or wait, I should have asked the parrots?"

Rhett felt the slicing of Mara's eyes—vulture's talons—sharp enough to cut a coconut husk.

Ok. Returning sarcasm might not have been the best move. He took a deep breath before apologizing. "Look Mara, I'm sorry. That came out wrong."

Mara's eyes softened—just a tad. "It's just, I'm worried and can't shake this feeling of ... of well, feeling like all this is going to bite back and bite hard. Can you at least assure me that you've asked the Sovereign about this plan?"

Rhett turned again to peer upriver. "Where is that boat; it should have been here by now."

"Rhett?" Mara asked again gently.

"I don't think He'd mind, Mara. It's a good plan. We can't ask the Sovereign about everything, can we?"

In the silence, Rhett stole a side glance back. Mara stared into the jungle darkness. "Please go back, Mara. Regardless of how safe I think it is, I'd feel better knowing you were home tonight."

"Yeah, I know the feeling," Mara whispered before disappearing in the direction of a neighboring tree.

Gone was Rhett's mood of anticipation. *I wish it was over now. She's right. I should've consulted the Sovereign. But what good would that have done; He hasn't answered any of my other prayers.*

The first glance at the approaching cargo boat pushed aside the rising guilt. Rhett whistled the warning for his Howler helpers to move into position. "Action time" he muttered, scurrying farther out onto the branch. With one arm firmly attached to a swinging vine and the stick in the other, he reminded himself to breathe. When the boat finally sailed alongside his tree, he leaped and landed with soft paws on the deck.

The man sitting at the helm hadn't even noticed his arrival. The open bottle of foul-smelling liquid on a cooler next to his chair probably had something to do with the man's incompetence as a watchman.

Rhett inched along the deck, careful to avoid stepping on the empty cans and plastic trash that littered the floor. Within a matter of seconds, Rhett had leaped onto the railing behind the man, took aim, and swung his stick for a solid connection with the man's head. The giant crumpled onto the floor like one of his sister's fur baby toys.

That taken care of, Rhett tossed the stick down and scampered over to the door. A few well-placed knots secured the latch. He put his ear to the door and couldn't hear any stirring. *With any luck, if there are more men down there, they'll sleep through the whole thing.*

Rhett then climbed to the highest spot on the boat, atop several large wooden crates. He waved his arms in a signal that the Howlers should swing across. Brun' and Brut' landed with thumps loud enough to wake a nesting mud frog. With an exasperated sigh, Rhett turned to inspect the waters over the railing. There they were, just as they had planned.

Surrounding the boat, swarms of otters watched and listened for the signals. While they couldn't carry the full weight of the crates, they could give them extra buoyancy and guide them to shore.

With one last look at the fallen man, just to make sure he slept soundly, Rhett leaped onto the nearest crate and motioned the brothers over. "Here, let's start with this one."

To the Prophet's surprise, they didn't say a word but used their massive forearms to maneuver the crate over the side of the boat. Startled by the sound of the splash, Rhett hissed to the monkeys. "Shhh. You don't want to wake any men below."

After placing his paw over his mouth to reiterate his instruction, he crept on tippy paws to the back of the boat and peered over the rail. *Did it come up? Will the crate float?* That was the big question. The one factor Rhett had been most concerned about. Bobbing to the surface, the wooden treasure box elicited a sigh of relief from the tense Prophet. The otters were on it like ticks on a deer—buoying the box toward shore.

Rhett bounded to the next box and looked for the brothers. "Time to move, guys." He whispered. "Let's get this done!" Together, the Howlers used shoulders the size of Kapok trunks to push the next crate to the edge and send another box into the Great River.

"Hey, stop that!" yelled a man poking his head out of the now open door. "Get off the boat!" The man stepped closer to the monkeys but paused when he saw his friend sprawled out asleep on the deck. He backed up a pace and picked up a stick, the same stick Rhett had brought from shore and had thoughtlessly abandoned with the trash on the decking floor.

Rhett looked from the man to the monkeys. *How did he get out?* Panic rose in his chest when he saw the white teeth of the Howler brothers. Both flashed him mocking smiles. He looked over at the door. The vine he had used to secure the latch was shredded, bit through. *Why would they chew the vine? They knew I tied it for a reason.*

The man backed up even farther, knelt, and reached down with his free hand into the compartment he had just come from. He drew out another stick, but this one didn't come from shore, this one was a fire stick.

Brun' and Brut' recognized the fire stick as well and began screeching loud enough to alarm all of Sanchia. There was a click as the man did something to his fire stick. The new sound set the monkeys off. They charged the man together, looking as if they intended to butt him off like they had the crate. The fire stick exploded. Bruno fell first—face down on the deck—arm stretched out reaching toward his brother.

"Brutus, stop!" Rhett yelled, hoping to deter the monkey from going any nearer to the fire stick. Brutus either didn't hear or didn't heed the warning. Baring his teeth, the monkey lunged at the man. The fire stick exploded a second time.

Blood now flowed from both brothers, enough that a small stream charted a course across the deck. Bruno had his eyes open and was moving his mouth as if trying to say something. Brutus wasn't moving at all.

The man turned toward the kinkajou on the railing. Regret was etched on the man's face, mirroring Rhett's own countenance. Before the fire stick could explode a third time, the Prophet bailed overboard.

112

Discussion Questions

1. Rhett chose not to heed Mara's warning. When others give us advice on what we should or shouldn't do, how do we determine whether to listen?

2. What is a good overall strategy for making big decisions?

Chapter

20

Words of Life

Giran." A voice called to him from the stillness of sleep. It sounded just like his father's. *Tirgato's back? Am I in the pit?* Fear paralyzed the jaguar, and he hesitated to raise even an eyelid. *Maybe the nightmare will go away.*

"Giran, get up." The voice whispered—closer this time. He could feel the breath in his ear. Reluctantly, Giran opened one eye. Sunlight poured into his cave around the shiny outline of his brother.

"How'd you get past the sentries … again?" Giran muttered, still trying to wake up.

Adan tilted his head. "It's difficult?"

Giran pulled up into a sitting position, licked his paws and wiped his face. Maybe it was thankfulness that his nightmare wasn't reality— it was Adan here and not Tirgato—but for the first time, he could say he wasn't afraid of his brother. On the contrary, he felt concerned. "Adan, you shouldn't be here. Your leg, the Prophet said to stay off it for a week, remember?"

"Of course, I remember, dull wit."

Well, he certainly has his sense of charm back.

Adan sighed and took a step as if to pace the opening only to wince when his weight shifted to his injured leg. "I need you to tell me more about the Sovereign. I think He's haunting me. It's all I could think about yesterday." The large jaguar circled and sat down next to Giran. "I wish you hadn't even sung that stupid song. Now it's stuck in my head—along with all its words."

Giran's ears perked up. "You know the words? How? I don't even know all the words."

Adan met his brother's eyes. "Raissa, your mom, used to sing the songs all the time. She wouldn't stop no matter how much Tirgato threatened. How could I not know the words?"

Giran tingled with the same excitement he felt anytime he heard something about his mother. Without remembering who he was talking to, he blurted, "Will you teach them to me? All the words, I mean."

Adan gave him an exasperated look. "Not now, Giran. Maybe sometime … later. Look, I need to know what you meant about the Sovereign. You said you'd tell me, but then you left." Adan squinted his eyes as if considering if Giran's offence was worth fighting over.

"I've been gone one day." Giran argued in self-defense.

"Anyway, you can tell me now." He gingerly licked his sore leg.

Giran stared at his brother, stared out the cave, then stared at the ceiling. Nothing came to mind. It was as if a giant wave from the Great River had crashed over his mind and cleared away all rational thought.

"Ahem." Adan coughed, making it clear he was more than ready for the explanation.

"Adan, I don't know what you want. The Sovereign forgave my mistakes when I asked, gave me peace, and helps me do things right."

"Like helping me get out of the trap? You said that was His doing, right?"

"Yeah, no offense, but I wouldn't have been that nice to you on my own."

Adan snorted. "You got too much of our dear father's blood in you for that."

Giran could only shrug. *Probably true.*

"So, how do you get the Sovereign to do what you want, give you all those things?"

Giran felt like a cornered capybara. He wanted to help his brother, but what could he say? Saloma had told him about the Sovereign and had made it seem so clear. "Ummm," is all that came out.

To Adan's credit, he didn't issue another snide comment about Giran's ineptness to explain. Instead, he just sighed and hung his head. Just when Giran was about to despair, a thought came to mind. "Adan, we need to go to Prophet Sam."

"What's up with you and Prophet Sam? I mean, I'm glad he was able to come and help with my leg and all, but before that, he never did one thing to help anyone. He's rather incompetent as far as Prophets go."

"How do you know? Has anyone ever given him a chance?"

Adan looked out of the cave into the light. "Not really, I guess. At least since I've been here."

"Just like the trap, he would have had to have been trained by the Prophet before him, and that training would have included Sovereign knowledge, right?"

The older jaguar wrinkled his nostrils as if he had just sat down near a pile of cow dung. "I guess so."

Giran jumped to all fours. "Well, let's go then."

"Just go—uninvited by Sam—with my weird questions about the Sovereign?"

"To Prophet Sam, and yes." Giran edged beside his brother. "Come on. I'll help you get up and walk. You start explaining how to get past the sentries."

***

Giran stared out his cave, and even without much of a moon, he saw things clearly for the first time since coming to Altura. He must keep his word to Rhett—return to Sanchia with the needed cats.

The Prophet had been reluctant to talk with them earlier that day as Giran had thought he might. He pulled the "I don't remember," bit like he did before, but Giran could see in his eyes the flash of understanding and knowledge of life. After some prodding, he finally answered Adan's questions. They all sat under the Guanandi tree as the ancient words of hope floated on the gentle afternoon breeze.

At first, Giran doubted they'd make any difference in his brother. How could they? Adan was as hardened a jaguar as Giran had ever known. Almost murdered his father, maybe helped kill the female cubs of their tribe. During most of Sam's explanation, Adan's expression was like stone, as cold and dead as Giran feared his heart to be. But when the Prophet mentioned the Sovereign giving creatures a new conscience as smooth and fresh as the sand on the shore, Adan broke down sobbing. Not a second later, Prophet Sam joined him. Both jaguar and anteater stood side by side under the Guanandi tree crying enough tears to flood the lowlands. *Of course, my eyes weren't exactly dry.*

Adan needed help getting home. The wound on his leg had opened and was leaving drops of blood along the path by the time they had reached the outskirts of Adan's community. But the jaguar didn't appear to be in any pain. His eyes were bright, and his tail wouldn't stop swaying back and forth. He had even thanked Giran for helping him—called him brother.

So here Giran sat, hours later, unable to fall asleep even though his ears drooped with exhaustion. *Too much to think about.* In addition to seeing his brother change right before his eyes like a multi-colored gecko, the talk about the Sovereign had reminded him of some things. *I need to keep my commitments first, even if it is hard, and even if Cora doesn't understand. Hopefully, she'll come with me. But if she doesn't, I must do what I promised I'd do.*

Giran closed his eyes. *I'll talk with her and Elder Ramiro in the morning. Annnddd, plan my trip home.*

Discussion Questions

1. Giran is a gifted encourager who believes the best in others. He was willing to give Prophet Sam a second chance and encourage his brother to find out about the Sovereign. How can you be an encourager to those around you?

2. Giran had trouble telling his brother how to find a relationship with the Sovereign. As Christians, it's important that we know how to show others the way of salvation. Below is a basic guide that you might want to memorize and be able to use if the situation presents itself.

A. **Admit** that you have broken God's laws, and you are a sinner. The penalty for sin is death, eternal death in a place called Hell.

    i.   Romans 3:23: "for all have sinned and fall short of the glory of God."

    ii.   Romans 6:23: "For the wages of sin is death, but the gift of God is eternal life in Christ Jesus our Lord."

B. **Believe** that Jesus Christ, the Son of God, died on the cross to pay the penalty for your sins and then rose again to life on the third day to declare that He is who He said He was – Almighty God, faithful Savior, Deliverer from death and the grave.

    i.   John 6:40: "For my Father's will is that everyone who looks to the Son and believes in him shall have eternal life, and I will raise them up at the last day."

C. **Confess** your sins to God, asking His forgiveness, and **Confess** Him as Lord of your life by committing to live your life in obedience to His commandments as given in His Holy Word, the Bible.

i.   Romans 10:9: "If you declare with your mouth, "Jesus is Lord," and believe in your heart that God raised him from the dead, you will be saved."

All scripture quotes are from NIV.

Chapter

21

Birth of Anarchy

Rhett swayed under the oppressive heat. Images appeared tilted or was he standing cockeyed? He was so dizzy, he couldn't tell. Sweat soaked his fur. His tail and ears stood at attention until the tips burned. Filling Rhett's nose, his mouth, his eyes, the smoke hung in gray wisps around his head. The fire closing in around him roared louder than a flash flood off the Great River.

"Mara? Where are you?" he screamed. "Answer me!" Her outline appeared in the smoke like a jungle apparition. "Mara, I'm coming." She faded into the gray vapor. "No, Mara!"

He tried to run, reached his paw out for a branch but missed. He was falling, falling, ..."

"Rhett, wake up!" Mara yelled in his ear while shaking his shoulder. "Rhett, I'm right here. Wake up!"

He opened his eyes. Mara was no longer a dim ghost but a better-than-bananas, beautiful kinkajou with lush fur and a shapely tail. He closed his eyes, savoring the image until she shook his wits back in order.

"Mara," he jerked to sitting. "Do you smell that? Do you hear a crackling sound?"

"No, Rhett. You were dreaming. It was just a bad dream." She cooed and petted his head as she would one of his twin siblings. He should have been embarrassed, should have told her to stop, but her touch felt so soft and gentle. *No need to hurt her feelings.*

Unfortunately, she stopped after a moment and backed away to sit opposite him on the Wimba platform.

Her grim look brought back the images from last night's failed venture. *Is she here to rub my nose in it?*

"Are you okay, Rhett?" she asked softly. "I mean, from last night. Are you hurt?"

Rhett couldn't decide between a 'yes' or 'no' to the two questions so ignored both. "Does everyone know? How it turned out, I mean."

Mara nodded. "News in this jungle travels fast."

Rhett grimaced. "Yep, faster than a falcon's dive."

"Why'd you do it, Rhett? Why didn't you at least ask the Sovereign first?"

Rhett shrugged. What could he say? "Look, I just thought it would work, that's all. And I have prayed, even if not specifically about last night. I've prayed over and over again about this famine and drought. He's not listening or if He is, He's not answering."

"Maybe His answer is 'wait.'" Mara whispered.

Her words hit him like a coconut from the canopy. *That does make sense. But then ...* "What if the Sovereign actually wants us to solve our own problems?"

Mara crossed her arms and tilted her head in a sassy, sideways position.

Rhett ignored the look and went on. "Really, what if He wants us to use the brains and resources He gives us, and we just continue to fail over and over again?"

The Prophet couldn't stand to look her in the eyes anymore. That was it. He knew it. The failure was his. He was responsible for not fixing the famine, for not having the medicine for Tomás, for harshly sentencing Dex, for losing the Howler brothers. Well, the brothers

121

weren't really his fault, even though he felt bad they had been killed on one of his missions.

Mara inched over to him and placed her paw on his knee, jolting him from any other rational thought. The pressure warmed more than his knee. Her paw rested so close to his. One little movement and he could wrap her paw in his.

"Rhett, you're not a failure."

Her words brought him back to ground level. He cleared his throat and hopefully, his errant thoughts. "Look, Mara, I'm sorry I didn't listen to you last night. You were right."

She looked shyly down at her other paw. "Thanks, Rhett. For saying that."

He moved his paw directly beside hers and touched the outside of her palm. She opened her paw slightly to allow him to slide his paw in. *I'm holding her paw; I'm holding her paw!* His thoughts bounced like crickets in the sunshine.

Blush river orchids blossomed in Mara's cheeks. Both tails swished, but their mouths stayed still for several minutes.

"Rhett," Mara broke the peace with a whisper. "Your mom told me about your dad."

Rhett jerked his paw away and sat up. "My dad? Why?" He stood and paced the branch. "Why would she tell you? She didn't have the right to do that."

Mara's eyes, that had misted after he pulled away, now shot bolts of fire. "Maybe she told me because it's her story too. "Actually if you ask, it is more her story than yours."

Rhett turned his back on her. Fast breathing made his nostrils flare in an unflattering way. "She should have at least told me first."

"Hmm." Scolded the angry female behind him. "*You* should have told me first."

Rhett shrugged.

Azul swooped down and landed on the platform. "Monkeys are coming—mad monkeys arriving soon," he announced before flying away. Birds knew everything. Rhett often wondered why they didn't rule the world. He was tempted to ponder such things, tempted to push his conversation with Mara out of his mind. But Mara was still here, and Elder Mateo and his cohorts were already halfway across the Sanctuary field.

"I'm going, Rhett." Mara stood and backed toward the tree trunk. He didn't turn around—didn't want her to see him upset.

Right before climbing to the Sanctuary ground, she said, "If it makes any difference, I don't care who your dad is or what he does. I wish you had believed that about me."

Rhett turned then to face her, to tell her he did know that about her. Maybe that would have been a lie. She was gone anyway, already well on her way across the brown field.

Rhett sighed. *How did it go so good—and then so bad—so quick?*

"Prophet," Mateo shouted between gasps for air as he approached the Wimba. Rhett didn't have the luxury at the moment to dwell on his relationship with Mara. He had business to deal with. Should he meet Mateo on the ground? No. At least with him perched on the Wimba platform, the overwhelming size difference didn't seem as threatening.

"You left them there…to die. You sit up there in that tree safe, but where are the brothers? Dead is where! And you killed them."

Rhett fought back the urge to roll his eyes. The elder was certainly laying it on thick. Not that he didn't feel bad about leaving Bruno and Brutus. But chances were, the fire stick killed them. What could he have done?

"Mateo." Rhett addressed the aged monkey softly, raising his palms to the stars, hoping to diffuse the situation. "I am sorry about your kin. It was not my intention that they get hurt in any way."

"You said your plan was monkey-proof. Remember?"

Mateo had a point. His plan obviously wasn't monkey-proof.

He breathed deep through his nostrils and tried again. "Did your informants tell you that Bruno or Brutus, I'm not sure which, bit through the rope – the rope that kept the man away while we worked.

Why, Mateo? Why did they purposely disobey my orders? Why would they intentionally set the man loose?"

Mateo deflated as if Rhett had kicked him in the gut. The Prophet couldn't help imagining that scenario and cringed. His entire leg would be swallowed in blubber.

The old monkey huffed. "I know nothing about that."

"Mateo, you assured me that the brothers would do just like I told them to. But when I had my back turned from them for a split second, they went and bit the man free. And then, I'm to blame when the whole thing goes rotten?"

"Who's to say they cut the rope? You didn't see it." The elder looked around at his posse of lesser monkey elders. "A kinkajou tied the knot. Anyone knows rodents can't tie a knot worth ant snot."

Rhett rolled his eyes then with no regret. True, kinkajous were not known for their knot-tying ability, but Rhett was not a normal kinkajou. And he certainly wasn't a rodent.

"Mateo, the vine was sliced through! Not undone – sliced. As in bit by razor-sharp Howler teeth. Now, again, why would they have done that?"

The elder shrugged non-committal like. "You should have protected them. It was your plan—your operation."

Rhett stared at the old monkey, hardly believing his ears. "How can I be held responsible if they did something incredibly stupid that ruined everything?"

"You were the one in charge. You're the Prophet. You should have paid more attention—made sure they understood what not to do. This would have never happened if Saloma had been in charge."

At this, the other monkeys howled in agreement. Fire coursed through Rhett's veins—his ears swelling to twice their normal size. "You're right, this wouldn't have happened, because you and the brothers would have actually listened to Saloma – a courtesy not yet given to me."

"We'll listen when you have something decent to say, something that may help us out of this famine. Fattima's right. We don't need a

Prophet. From now on, we'll rule ourselves. You keep your tail out of our business, and we'll stay out of yours."

Rhett didn't try to hold in his snort. "You rule yourselves? You couldn't keep the order for one season, much less solve the food shortage issues."

"We'll see about that … Rhett." Mateo and company clawed at the ground and then spun around to charge back across the field. Dust rose like a cloud into the Wimba. As the monkeys stormed out of the Sanctuary, Rhett tried to shout parting snide remarks but could only sneeze in their wake.

Discussion Questions

1. Have you ever felt as if God was telling you to wait in response to one of your prayers? When and how did you deal with the waiting time?

2. Instead of keeping his anger in check and working to diffuse the situation, Rhett allows a group to walk away from his authority and the Sovereign's set order. What are some ways he could have handled the situation better?

Chapter

22

Truth Revealed

"I told you for the last time," growled Ramiro. "Cora will not be leaving Altura."

"Sir, I gave my word." Giran pleaded, trying to get the elder to understand his torn loyalties. As soon as the words left his mouth, Cora looked up, tears in her eyes.

Giran hung his head, the weight of guilt almost too much to bear. *Why did I promise what I couldn't do?*

"Elder Ramiro, I want Cora to come with me, yes, but what I really want is for all of you to relocate. Please won't you consider migrating to Sanchia? There's more game in Sanchia right now than ants in Altura. Plus, there are ready dens waiting for you."

"Why would I leave, Giran? We have everything we need here— game aplenty. If you want cats so badly, go ask Vinícius. Please take as many of his cats with you as you like!"

"There's history there." Giran said in a voice barely north of a whisper.

"History?" The old elder raised his eyebrow.

"Vinícius' tribe won't go back to Sanchia."

"Why not? Have you asked them? That's where they're from. Have them reclaim their homes, eat the plentiful food, and leave us alone."

"They won't go back with me."

Ramiro didn't say anything—just stared—waiting for an explanation.

Giran exhaled. "Tirgato was my father. He's the reason they left in the first place. There's no way they would follow me home to Sanchia."

Elder Ramiro growled at the mention of Tirgato's name, which wasn't an uncommon response. The old jaguar had a reputation, at least in the nearby regions, of being notoriously ruthless.

"Adan?"

"My half-brother by Tirgato."

Pacing the dirt-packed floor of the cave, Ramiro looked like a ripe passion fruit about to bust and blow seeds into the canopy. "Why didn't you tell us this before? You chose to deceive us after we welcomed you."

Giran shook his head. "It wasn't my intention to mislead. I …. I didn't know, you said I was finally home. You said so yourself, because of Raissa. I guess I just hoped it wouldn't matter if it came up."

"Wouldn't matter? That my daughter cares for the son of the most evil jaguar since Ignacio."

Giran thought about disputing that point. For all his faults, Tirgato wasn't as bad as Ignacio. Ignacio was a nightmare known for eating cubs for the fun of it. Ramiro's face was twisted in anger and his tail taut. There were better times to argue Tirgato's limited merits.

The heated discussion had attracted a company of jurors in the courtyard. All the eyes trained on him made him feel like a cricket who had foolishly landed in the middle of a tree frog colony. Elder Ramiro turned tail to Giran and approached the surrounding jaguars.

As the cats parted, the old jaguar looked over his shoulder, but his gaze didn't make it all the way to Giran's eyes. "The sun is just now showing its face. Be gone before it sleeps again."

Giran hung his head. Responding to the edict would be pointless. It was clear and sure in the presence of witnesses.

Giran glanced at Cora who was lying nearby. She had been silent during the whole tense exchange. Tears flowed down her petite jaw and sparkled in the morning light like jewels flowing down Rainbow Falls. His heart ripped in two. "Cora, I'm so sorry. I didn't mean any of this. I shouldn't have promised you I wouldn't leave. I ... I just so wanted to stay. Cora looked down at the moist dirt between her outstretched forelegs but didn't say anything. "I'll be back, Cora. Let me take care of business in Sanchia, and I'll come back for you. Okay?"

Giran lay down beside her as the sun rose above the cliffs. With nothing more to entertain them, the crowd dispersed, leaving the two jaguars alone to grieve.

✳✳✳

The tiny crescent moon disturbed the darkness about as much as a baby minnow would the waves of the Great River. No shadows swayed along the path. A stillness akin to death blanketed the trail. Giran's eyes grew to the size of lily pads, and the fur along the back of his neck stood at attention. Others lurked nearby—he was sure of it. He heard the occasional rustle of grass—smelled the cat musk carried on the midnight breeze.

Why are so many jaguars hunting tonight? And so early in the evening? He didn't voice his questions but kept his nose to the dirt. He had most likely been spotted but for whatever reason, ignored. Okay with him. The quicker he made it out of Altura and into Cantiga, the better. Maybe he would make quick work of persuading some of Raissa's kin to come back to Sanchia.

"Pssst. Giran. Over here."

The whisper came from under the brush on the side of the path. Giran stopped in his paw tracks—undecided as to what to do.

"Giran." The voice now louder and more insistent. "Get over here."

Eyebrows raised with skepticism, Giran tip-pawed off the path and behind the bordering bush.

"I couldn't stop them, Giran. They're intent on taking over the caves."

"Adan. You really should stay still if that leg's going to heal. What are you even talking about? Caves?"

His brother growled in irritation. "Listen, Elder Vicínius pulled all the warriors together at sunset for a conference. He's decided that trying to capture a few of Ramiro's females one at a time isn't working fast enough."

"Giran, I'm not following. Fast enough for what? I thought you said your tribe took the females because they needed mates. So, why the sudden hurry?"

"You're partly right – we do need mates. But that need coincides with the goal of taking over the cliffs and moving away from the border. He's merging the tribes tonight, under his leadership"

"I don't understand."

"Look, I don't have time to explain it all. Vicínius is on his way right now with a large posse to kill or run off all the males, starting with Elder Ramiro."

"But why? Why are they killing their own?"

"Their own, Giran? Ramiro's tribe never made us feel welcome here. By the time I found Vicínius and the rest of my old tribe after Tirgato kicked me out of Sanchia, Ramiro was already wanting to get rid of us. They shoved us into the corner of Altura that they didn't want themselves. When we needed them, they didn't share mates; they thought themselves too good for us."

Giran narrowed his eyes. "You wouldn't have needed females if you had let the young ones live."

Snarling, Adan spit a response. "Don't believe every rumor you hear, Giran. For whatever reason, our tribe has had only two females born in the last five seasons. The last one—barely out of nursery—was fought over so many times, she almost caused a tribal split."

Giran hung his head. He should have verified his story before spouting it off like fact. "I'm sorry—I assumed the worst."

"Hadn't you noticed that Ramiro's tribe is full of female cubs? Do they kill their males at birth?"

Giran shook his head. He had wondered about the lack of male cubs but didn't make the connection that he blamed Adan's tribe of the same atrocious evil that could be put also on Ramiro's.

"I misjudged, Adan. Forgive me?"

To his credit, Adan nodded, and that was the end of it.

"Anyway," Adan continued, "Vicínius can't or won't wait any longer for those cliffs."

"Cliffs? I thought he wanted females."

"Both Giran! He wants—no needs—both. If it was just females, we would recruit from other regions like Ramiro does."

"So, Vicínius wants one jaguar tribe, under him, living on the highland." Giran voiced, understanding dawning. "I can try to warn Ramiro, Adan, but how far ahead of me are the warriors?"

Not far. If you go directly through the brush and not along the path, you could beat them. If not, there'll be a slaughter tonight."

"But why, why tonight?"

"It's partly my fault. They found out about my leg and the trap. The attacks from man have been relentless lately. They're moving farther and farther into our territory. I escaped from the trap, but the man came and put two more in its place. Who knows how many more traps are hiding around in the brush? Vinícius' youngest son went missing last night, and that was the last coconut. We must get away from man. The cliffs are our only, or at least our best option."

Now understanding the gravity of the situation, Giran shook in anticipation of the run to come. "I gotta warn Cora's family. Adan, go as fast as you can, but not too fast. Don't hurt yourself! But hurry and get the Prophet. Maybe he can find some way to help too."

Adan shook his head. "You and that Prophet again."

Giran gave his brother a half smile before he turned south toward the caves. He needed to fly like Rhett if had any hope of winning the race against Vicínius' warriors.

Discussion Questions

1. Giran believed the atrocious rumor that Adan's tribe killed their female cubs. According to 1 Corinthians 13:4-7, how should have Giran treated his brother?

   "Love is patient, love is kind. It does not envy, it does not boast, it is not proud. It does not dishonor others, it is not self-seeking, it is not easily angered, it keeps no record of wrongs. Love does not delight in evil but rejoices with the truth. It always protects, always trusts, always hopes, always perseveres." – 1 Cor. 13:4-7 (NIV)

2. What are some ways in this chapter that Adan is already showing signs of the Sovereign's gift of new life?

Chapter

23

Cats and Bats

Giran sprinted back to Cora's home as strong and straight as a falcon's dive. He could sense jaguars on both sides of him in the darkness—heard them keeping pace—gaining on him even. But then they fell back as if not sure whether to engage him or stay the order for a tight unit attack. Giran kept his nose pointed straight and only slowed when the first sentry came into sight. Out of breath, he could only manage, "Attack!"

The sentry stared at him wide-eyed. Giran struggled to breathe and yell again. "Attack coming. Go!" Finally, the guard woke from his stupor. Just for added emphasis, Giran added, "What is wrong with you? Go for help." Giran gasped for more air. "Tell the others!"

The warning, this time effective, sent the sentry sprinting to the courtyard while sounding the warning call. Still relatively early in the evening, the jaguars were stretching from naps, milling around the camp chatting with neighbors, and discussing the hunts to come before sunrise. All came to attention with the warning call, and many more emerged from the caves surrounding the courtyard.

Other sentries joined the group from the outlying woods and plied the guard who sounded the alarm with questions and accusations. While trotting from his den entrance, Ramiro's eyes locked on Giran standing near the outskirts of the camp. From the narrowed slits, Giran could only imagine the growl that boiled behind the elder's clenched teeth.

The jaguars had barely assembled in the center when the attacking warriors bounded out of the surrounding brush into the courtyard. Each jaguar seemed to have a target and surged for their individual opponent without giving any time for Ramiro's tribe to organize.

No one charged Giran. *What should I do—who should I help?* None of the females engaged the warriors. Instead, they nervously paced in front of their cave entrances. All except Cora. She leapt into the fray to help one of her cousins against an oversized opponent. "Cora, get back. What are you doing?" Giran yelled in her direction to no avail. *She's no match for these guys.*

Giran sprinted in her direction, dodging several skirmishes and jumping over two jaguars caught in a roll combat. The large jaguar Cora attacked had managed to either claw or bite out her cousin's right eye and now turned toward her. He had a vile grin on his face as if enjoying the prospect of tangling with the Princess of the tribe.

Giran never slowed from his sprint but rammed full force into the jaguar's left shoulder, bowling him over onto the dirt. He instantly went for the jugular, not thinking it wise to prolong a fight he had little chance of winning. But the jaguar recovered from the surprise attack with lightning speed and jerked his head around at the last second to deflect Giran's bite. Both jaguars leapt to their feet and began the war dance: two cats at face-off, hissing and sidestepping in a circular motion.

Cora, to Giran's relief, backed off a few feet and didn't show signs of interfering. She scurried over to help her cousin, blind now, one eye from injury and one from the copious outpouring of blood. The thought that Cora was safe for the moment streaked through his consciousness, enabling him to focus on the fight.

The other jaguar was a seasoned warrior—old but not gray—large but not fatty—quick but not squirrely in his movements. His posture exuded the confidence of an experienced elder.

"So, Tirgato again. It's been a while." The elder said in a mocking tone.

Giran wasn't sure if he was actually being mistaken for his father or if the warrior was simply baiting him. Either way, he figured it safer to keep his mouth shut. Taunts were given to rattle opponents, and Giran wasn't green enough to fall for that one.

When the other jaguar realized that his distraction tactics wouldn't work, he lunged at Giran to mount him with his left foreleg. Giran shifted enough that the mount failed but flinched as four deep gashes raked his side. The jaguar's exhaled breath breezed his shoulder, and a missed bite rattled just behind his ear. Giran sidestepped again and tried to backpedal before the next lunge.

The elder didn't allow him a breather but attacked on the bounce, this time a low frontal attack to the jugular. Giran shifted all his weight to his hind legs in barely enough time to lift his front legs in defense. He deflected the charge and claimed an aggressive attack hold on the elder's back neck. Both collapsed under the combined weight.

Before either could react and launch their next move, a piercing sound—both shocking and painful—stunned them both. Without hesitation, both jaguars abandoned the fight in search of the bigger threat. From above, a massive, living cloud of evil descended on Altura.

Thousands—no millions of bats—slipped into the courtyard, screeching, and hissing, and diving at the bewildered cats. Bat guano pelted the jaguars' golden fur like white rain. While the vibrations pulsing through the air agonized the jaguars' ears, the steady beat of wings brought terror to their hearts. Most of the cats hid their faces between their forelegs and attempted to drown out the sound with front paws pressed against their ears.

The bats flew over the field for what seemed like hours even though the drumming and vibrating made it impossible to reason the passing of time. The bravest of cats were cowering by the time the stream of rodent birds thinned. Giran peeked above his sheltering arm and saw the field covered with jaguars lying flat on the ground with their heads and tails tucked.

Prophet Sam stood on top of a boulder that stretched out over the courtyard. The anteater Prophet looked down his nose at the mass of cats, silently daring any of them to move. He looked different though Giran couldn't put his paw on why. It was the same anteater—but not the same Prophet. There was nothing pitiful about Sam today, nothing about him that would elicit a feeling of "Wow, I'm glad I'm not him." On the contrary, the way his beady eyes darted around the field, Giran couldn't imagine anyone not being afraid of the Prophet. *Funny—afraid of an anteater.*

Adan leaned against Sam's boulder, protected by the rock from the onslaught of bats. At the Prophet's paw raise, Adan limped forward. Raising his head, he roared an ear-splitting call that rivaled the intensity of the millions of bats and was sharp enough to strip the silver scales off a hatchet fish.

"The fighting must cease!" yelled the Prophet as if anyone dared still spar. "Each tribe…"

"Father!" yelled Cora, interrupting the Prophet and taking off across the field of jaguars. Elder Ramiro lay in a pool of blood with Vinícius standing over him.

Discussion Questions

1. Giran said of Prophet Sam, "It was the same anteater—but not the same Prophet." Why the change in Prophet Sam?

2. 2 Corinthians 5:17 says, "Therefore, if anyone is in Christ, the new creation has come: The old has gone, the new is here!" (NIV) When you became a Christian, what differences did you notice in your heart and life?

135

24

Son of
the Sovereign

R amiro's blood dripped from Vinícius' jaw. Of all the jaguars, Vinícius had recovered first from the onslaught of bats. The elder kept shifting his attention from the departing winged rodents, to Ramiro, to the Prophet, to his clan sprawled out on the field. His forehead was furrowed with countless grooves. Confusion was clearly not an emotion the elder seemed to be accustomed to or tolerated with patience. *Will he snap at any moment, ignore the Prophet, and continue the attack?*

Cora obviously didn't care what Vinícius thought. She butted him away from her father and fell on her knees by Ramiro. She licked the blood streaming from his neck and cooed softly as if tending a cub.

Vinícius looked down at Cora crying and desperately attending to her father's injury. The old jaguar sighed and diverted his eyes to study the ground. His shoulders slumped as if he had been the one defeated.

"Enough fighting." Prophet Sam commanded in a lower tone. "There must be peace among the jaguars. You are one family, princes among the cats of Altura. Your strength depends on your willingness to pursue oneness in purpose, oneness in mission, oneness in family. To thrive, you must learn to live together—no more this family or that tribe. You must become one."

Prophet Sam paused for a breath—everyone else seemed to be holding theirs, watching the anteater with fierce intensity.

"In Altura, there are many factions: otters split by color, marsh deer by size, monkeys by who knows what petty distinction. The day of separation in this jungle is over. The jaguars will lead the way by being the model of an integrated community. The time has come for change. The jaguars will be united starting today."

Vinícius interrupted. "Who are you, Sam, to tell us how to live? When did you decide to play the Prophet?"

Adan narrowed his eyes and issued a slight growl. Vinícius shifted his attention to Adan. "And you, son of Tirgato, I always knew you were trouble, but I didn't think you were a traitor." Adan's ears flattened, and his shoulders tensed. He took a few hobbled steps in the elder's direction.

"Father, stay with me." Cora pleaded, heedless of the exchange going on behind her.

Giran walked to stand beside Cora. Ramiro's eyes were still open but cloudy with pain. His neck, chin, and chest were covered with an oozing layer of crimson. There was so much blood—Giran couldn't see the exact wound line.

Giran looked up at Sam. "Prophet, can you do something? Will you do something to help Ramiro?"

The anteater Prophet surprised everyone with a smile. Giran tilted his head, trying to understand the strange creature. *Surely he's not mocking us now?* But before anyone could lash out in anger, Sam answered. "I had a dream yesterday. The first in a long time."

Giran didn't understand what Sam meant, not exactly, but both ears and tail perked high in anticipation. Rhett had told him of his dreams and even some of Saloma's. Something was coming—and judging by Sam's goofy grin—something good.

The other jaguars showed no signs of excitement over Sam's proclamation of a dream. They stared at him climbing down the side of the boulder like he was two bananas shy of a bunch. The small crowd on the field between the Prophet and Ramiro parted to let Sam through. When he reached Cora's side, he laid a paw on her leg—for he couldn't quite reach her shoulder—and gently pushed her aside.

Sam looked down at Ramiro and studied him for a minute as the mass of jaguars pressed in to watch the unfolding drama. When stillness prevailed in the surrounding circle, the Prophet reached out as if to touch Ramiro but then drew back his paw as if pricked by a thorn. Sam stared at the elder a few more seconds before raising up on both hind legs.

While rubbing his two front paws together, he cleared his throat and began to speak. It wasn't loud but sufficient for all crowded near to hear. "By the Sovereign's will and power, Ramiro, you're healed." The audacity of the statement elicited a collective gasp from the jaguars. No one moved a hair or even breathed. All eyes locked in on the elder lying motionless in the dust.

Unfortunately, Ramiro didn't say anything or even move a twitch.

A few of the jaguars milling around the outer ring of the crowd snickered. Giran shot them a dangerous look from over the crowd of golden hides, but inside he fretted. *What is Sam doing? Why'd he say something like that if he wasn't sure it'd work?*

Sam came back down to all fours and nudged Ramiro's side with his snout. "This isn't the time for sleeping, Ramiro," he declared to the still jaguar in a booming voice. "Wake up and get up."

The Prophet's nose nudge must have jarred the old jaguar back to reality. He blinked a few times before carefully raising his head and catching sight of Sam. Eyes trained on the Prophet—Ramiro stood. Cora let out a cry and circled twice in excitement before licking her father's face. Sam watched them for a moment with a smile before turning away.

The crowd of stunned and silent jaguars parted again as the Prophet walked back toward his boulder. Giran wondered about his

138

next move along with probably every creature present. *He certainly has their respect now.*

"Now, as I said before, this feuding between jaguarshas gone on long enough. Along with showing me Ramiro's healing, the Sovereign revealed to me his plan for your tribes. Listen carefully, heed His words, and all will go well with you."

Sam paused and glared in Vinícius' direction. The older jaguar met his eyes and nodded his head. *He's going to listen. I can't believe it.* Giran felt like leaping in the air and doing circles just like Cora had. But before he could celebrate, the Prophet started up again.

"Man has become increasingly aggressive over the past few seasons to the point that the eastern lowlands are not safe for the jaguars. All families must live in the caves."

Vinícius' ears perked at the news. He glanced over at Cora's dad to gauge his response. Ramiro's face was blank, revealing nothing beyond total focus on Sam.

The Prophet continued. "That being said. There's not enough den space or game in the highlands to shelter both existing tribes. Half of you must leave Altura."

The jaguars stirred at these words, but no one dared speak against the Prophet—not yet anyway—not in his presence.

"And the half to leave must come from both tribes. Ramiro, your tribe has an abundance of females. Not a healthy situation. Vinícius you're in the same state, only opposite. The Sovereign has done this to prepare you for this time. The two tribes must merge."

Vinícius cleared his throat and claimed the attention of the assembly. "Where would the other half go? What are you saying?"

"Half of you will leave with Giran and go back to Sanchia. His region is in great need of cats. There you will find an abundance of food and ready-made dens."

"Yeah," growled Vinícius. "Dens built seasons ago by our own sweat and then denied us by his father. Do you expect us now to follow a son of Tirgato back to his home region? That's suicide!"

Many among the crowd grunted their approval. Giran hung his head. There was nothing he could say in his own defense. He was the son of Tirgato.

Adan spoke up. "My brother is different. He's …"

Vinícius interrupted, "One son of the devil speaks for the other."

Adan cleared his throat and stared at Vinícius until the silence settled like an oppressive weight on the backs of those listening. When the tension was almost too heavy to bear, Adan answered in a tone no one dared argue with. "He is no longer the son of Tirgato. He is a son of the Sovereign."

Tears threatened to flow as Giran looked up at Adan. "My brother spoke up for me. And he's right. I am a son of the Sovereign."

"Vinícius," the Prophet said, "don't be a fool and judge the sons by the deeds of the father." At first, the eyes of the old jaguar shot bolts of lightning at Sam. Without flinching, the Prophet met his gaze and held it until a lone stray bat dipped into the clearing. When the winged rodent landed on the anteater's shoulders, Vinícius dropped his head in acquiescence.

An awkward silence fell over the crowd. Sam took his time before speaking again. "Adan is right. Giran follows the Sovereign—unlike his father before him. He will lead you well. As a matter of fact, Giran will not only lead you back to Sanchia—he will be your head elder."

At these words, even Giran's mouth hung open. *I'm too young to be a head elder. What is Sam doing?*

The Prophet looked down at Giran and gave him a smirk as if he could read his doubts. Giran wondered—not for the first time—if a Prophet could read a creatures' thoughts.

Before any of the jaguars could object and attempt to make the claim that Giran leading them would be ludicrous, Sam spoke again. "This was part of the dream. It is unusual, given his age and background, but the Sovereign was clear." At the mention of his dream, most of the jaguars nodded their heads in acceptance.

Vinícius, you will stay here in Altura. You will not go back to Sanchia but will have the responsibility of choosing half of your warriors to go with Giran."

The elder didn't openly protest this time to the Prophet's words but did yawn with great demonstration as if the whole process was overly taxing.

Prophet Sam turned his snout towards Ramiro who still stared back at the anteater with a wide-open mouth. The elder hadn't said a word or wavered in his attention.

"Ramiro, you will leave Altura with half of your current tribe and half of Vinícius'. Will you follow Giran's lead and accept his headship?"

The silence that followed was louder than any rainy-day frog chorus. Ramiro broke his stare with Sam long enough to look at Giran, then at Cora. When he turned back to the Prophet, he declared, "I will. The Sovereign has my word."

Breaths were exhaled around camp that the jaguars didn't know they were holding. Everyone seemed to wake up from a long nap at the same time and the jaguars—who had tried to kill one another just moments before—helped each other up from the dirt. Some even helped mend the other's wounds.

The Prophet climbed down from the boulder and approached Adan. He motioned with his snout for the jaguar to come with him. The two walked toward the edge of the camp, deep in private conversation. Giran moved closer to the two, hoping to listen in. But to his dismay, all he heard before they ducked into the brush was, "Adan, I have a job just for you."

Discussion Questions

1. What kind of petty differences in our world separate people from one another? What does the Bible say about this issue?

2. Timothy was chosen to be a leader in the Christian church even though he was young because of his Godly attributes. 1 Timothy 4:12 says, "Don't let anyone look down on you because you are

young, but set an example for the believers in speech, in conduct, in love, in faith and in purity." (NIV) How can you be an example to older members of the church body?

Chapter
25

Covenant Ceremony

Golden rays from a setting sun spotlighted the circle of jaguars at the base of what was now known as Prophet's Rock. Most of the cats had never witnessed a covenant ceremony, only heard about the ancient ritual from the elders. But sense the renewal of the Prophet, a ceremony once considered old-fashioned now held a measure of intrigue. Even a few of Vinícius' tribe came for the ceremony, including Vinícius in a show of diplomacy. But it was Adan's presence that warmed the groom's heart the most.

They had hunted together the last few evenings and talked about things that Giran would have never dreamed they would share. Adan had taught him the words to Raissa's favorite songs, many of which brought tears to both jaguars. Giran had a chance to share with his brother a little of what it was like growing up with just Tirgato. Together they mourned their lost cubhood.

It was sad irony that after all their missed seasons, they would find each other only to be separated again after a few days. Adan had explained the conversation he had had with Prophet Sam in detail to Giran. The Prophet had asked Adan to go on a special assignment, and his brother had agreed. It was a good job for Adan. But the parting was still sad.

Sam had asked Adan to be an ambassador for Altura. Included in that role would be the task of sharing his story: what the Sovereign had done in his life. Many creatures in the surrounding jungle regions had forgotten about the Sovereign. Not only could they not live a life of blessing without that knowledge, but they needed to hear and accept the peace only the Sovereign could bring.

Giran looked over at Adan, who lay still in the last vestiges of sunlight, struggling not to nap. He chuckled at the memory of Adan questioning Sam's sanity to his face. When the Prophet had explained Adan's new job, he had asked, "Are you crazy? Don't you know who my father is?"

Sam was quick to assure Adan that he did in fact know, and that it would benefit the Sovereign's son to speak less and listen more. The Prophet went on to explain to a humbled Adan that the past would be only a part of his story—a part that would show others the offered forgiveness of their Creator.

Unfortunately, Adan's new job would have him traveling all over the rainforest. Giran hoped that his journeys would bring him to Sanchia on occasion.

Adan's tail swished him hard in the side. "Pay attention, brother, or I'll steal her yet." He threatened with a smirk.

Giran didn't bother to reply, couldn't reply, his breath stollen by the vision of Cora walking with her father toward Prophet's Rock. She was veiled in the fading sunlight. *Surely she's a vision from the Sovereign.* But the vision looked up and glanced shyly at Giran. His forelegswent weak. Sweat dripped off his ears. He whispered to his brother. "Are you hot? I feel like a sunbathing iguana." He panicked—felt like crumpling to the dirt under the pressure and turned red at the thought. He heard Adan chuckle and sensed vaguely that he was the source of much amusement for his brother.

Elder Ramiro and the angel walking beside him reached Prophet's Rock. Giran felt Adan nudge his hind leg, and he remembered to move into position at Cora's side. Their long tails sought each other and intertwined in perfect unison.

The Prophet cleared his throat, and the family of jaguars gathered closer. The many swishing of tails sounded like a gentle breeze across the canopy palms.

"Assembled Jaguars, Giran and Corazón desire to enter into a covenant relationship for the purpose of establishing a Sovereign blessed family. Does anyone present have a problem with that?"

No one answered, but the scowl Adan turned on the crowd could have wilted a ragweed.

"Good." Boomed the Prophet from high on his boulder. "In that case: Giran, Corazón – sing away."

Giran glanced shyly at Cora, but she kept her eyes down. They had written their song, practiced their song, but now the words floated away like capricious butterflies. He coughed, trying to clear the wasteland pebbles lodged in his throat. Cora snuck a peek his way, and when their eyes met, she smiled ever so slightly. Rising from the heart, Giran found his words.

(Giran)
Come my friends and listen
for an adventure begins today.
A tale full of promise
A tale full of hope
A tale of two joined the Sovereign's way.

Covenants are binding
For life promise is the Sovereign's will
Will for family, joy, peace
Will for tribes free of fear
Will for dens no predator dare kill

In front of witnesses
Dear Cora, I give my solemn vow
A vow when in plenty

A vow in fear and drought
A vow as long as life dare allow

(Together)
We will live and work together
Knowing joy and sometimes sorrow
Not giving up on each other
As we look for each tomorrow

(Cora)
Dear Giran, I promise
that I'll always be faithful and true
True when I'm sick or well
True when you're gone or home
True and faithful as the morning dew

The years will come and go
Our tails will sag, our fur will turn gray
Gray from years filled with fun
Gray from tears shed in pain
Gray from memories made each passing day

(Together)
May we keep this blessed covenant
Be helpful, devoted, and true.
We pray our den be filled with joy
As one entwined instead of two

At the end of the song, all the jaguars roared their loudest cries. Tears flowed down many golden jaws and not just from the feminine cats. The crowd milled around at the base of Prophet's rock, grooming one another and fellowshipping. There was much talk about the ceremony—and song in particular—as well as jibes and jokes directed toward the nervous groom.

After enduring a number of playful neck bites and tail slaps from his guests, Giran sought out Prophet Sam from among the crowd. The anteater had come down off his boulder and stood at the edge of the woodline, staring at him. Giran tilted his head and quickly made his way to his side.

"Thank you, Prophet Sam, for coming and …"

"Giran, I had another dream this morning."

Giran's heart dropped. Prophet's dreams could be good or bad. Either way they tended to change situations, and right at this moment, Giran felt pleasantly comfortable.

Sam continued. "It wasn't as detailed as I would like, but the gist was that you need to leave Altura right away, as in now. Don't delay any longer. You're needed in Sanchia."

"Is something wrong?" Giran's tail shot out with the question.

"Like I said, it was hazy—literally cloudy with a mass of smoke. I woke with my eyes watering and the fiery impression to speed you and your new tribe on your way."

Giran had hoped to spend a few more days with his brother. And what would Cora think about leaving right after their covenant ceremony? He looked over his shoulder for his new bride. He didn't have to look far. She lay on the grass, not a tail length away with a sly grin on her face. Her stealth skills as a huntress were definitely going to keep him on his paws. She gave him a slight nod, telling him what he needed to know.

"We'll leave at high moon." He said with no hesitation.

Discussion Questions

1. Have you ever met someone who God called to be a missionary to another country? Why do you think they sacrifice home and comfort to tell others about Jesus?

2. Malachi 2:14 refers to marriage as a covenant. What is a covenant, and what does that mean for marriage? "…she is your partner, the wife of your marriage covenant." Malachi 2:14 (NIV)

Chapter

26

If the Tail Trips

"They're at it again." declared Elder Horado, one of the few elders in attendance at the council. "They're probably there right now. It makes the third evening this week."

Rhett should feel a sense of gloating because he had been right concerning the monkeys. They couldn't rule themselves. But pride wasn't the emotion plaguing Rhett; it was guilt chasing at his tail, doubts, and fear of what his actions may have started.

He looked over the scant crowd. How soon before these creatures would abandon his rule as well? The anteaters no longer looked him straight in the eye, and the beavers huddled in the back, whispering to themselves. Even the marsh deer stared at the moonlit clouds, as if fearing they would turn into giant coconuts and drop from the sky.

Rhett peered over the creatures' heads at the sparse grass surrounding the Wimba. *Maybe they would be better without me? I can't help them. The food's almost gone, and I'm out of ideas. Not that my ideas ever go well anyway.*

"Ahem." Horado cleared his throat.

In panic Rhett searched the marsh deer's expression, trying to decipher what the elder had just said. Having pity on him, the elder repeated. "Have you heard from the elders of Placero?"

"I heard from their ambassadors yesterday." Rhett studied his paws. "I was going to bring that up at this meeting."

"You must reign in the monkeys!" Elder Renzo of the peccary clan spoke up. "If not, the northern regions will attack, and then we'll all suffer for their breach in conduct." A large snort punctuated the passion in his voice.

Rhett sighed. "How do you propose I do that, Elder? It's hard to expect them to go hungry and not at least attempt to gather food for their little ones."

Elder Horado looked up at him in surprise. "Are you saying we should break our treaty with Placero and gather on their land?"

"No! That's not what I mean." Rhett massaged a throbbing temple with one paw and reached for his tail with the other. "We're not to raid other lands, … but it's hard not to." The faces underneath him showed more confusion than squirrels in school.

A whisper from one of the beavers in the back—a whisper loud enough to be heard by every attendee—shook the floundering Prophet. "Now he sounds like Fattima."

Rhett recovered his voice with a sudden surge of anger. "Ha!" exclaimed the kinkajou, stomping on his hard wooden perch. "I knew she was behind this. I bet she's been leading the monkeys astray for weeks."

All the creatures, including Elder Horado, rolled their eyes in unison. "Rhett," he said in a calming tone, "I don't think another snake hunt would be a great idea right now."

"But don't you see? She disrupted the food shipment, influenced the monkeys to disobey simple instructions, and now she's completely turned them against me." Looking out at the scant crowd, he motioned with an open paw, "She's influenced more than the monkeys."

The elder looked around at his fellow elders and answered. "She's been talking to the other creatures, sure, but most realize she's just spewing bitter berries."

Renzo the peccary spoke up again. "From what I heard, Prophet, it was you who told Mateo to go his own way. How is that Fattima's fault?"

Rhett didn't answer. He beat the Wimba platform with his tail, blaming Fattima more with every thump.

Elder Cletus, one of the beavers from the back, elbowed a few peccary, anteaters, capybara, and marsh deer out of his way and approached the Wimba. "Prophet, it seems to me that you're going about this the wrong way. Where we beavers come from, in the far northern regions, we have a saying. "If the tail trips, chew it off."

Rhett instinctively reached for his own tail, guarding it against such a gruesome suggestion.

"Naw," the elder harrumphed and batted his tail against the ground. "Not *your* tail, the snake."

Rhett squinted his eyes. "Snakes don't have tails."

Elder Cletus breathed deep. "Forget the saying. The point is: Fattima wants her way, she's causing problems, let her go."

"I'd love it if she left!"

"No, you still don't understand. Fattima hangs out in the northern region near the monkeys, right?"

"Yeah." Rhett answered warily, unclear where the beaver was going.

"Well, no one else really uses those cliffs much anyway. Let Fattima, and the monkeys for that matter, do what they want, if they agree to stay in that region."

Rhett cocked his head, absorbing the elder's suggestion.

"You mean give her the northern region?"

"Well, not really, not official, just temporary like until things settle down. That way she backs off and can do whatever snakes want to do. And you're happy not dealing with her or the monkeys. A treaty sorta."

Rhett had to admit that the idea had merit. He hadn't been able to find Fattima, much less control her. Maybe giving in a little wouldn't be too bad – keep the peace and all. But ….."What if she won't agree to stay in the northern region?"

"At that point, you would have the clear and full support of all the elders to discipline her as you see fit. She would clearly be outside her boundaries."

Most of the other elders grinned and grunted with enthusiasm. The anteaters nodded so vigorously that they made oval dents in the dirt with their noses.

"What about the raids? You know the monkeys won't stop raiding."

Elder Cletus laughed. "Tell the Placero ambassadors of the temporary fissure and mention to them exactly where they can find the stolen food stores. Let them take care of the raiding in whatever way they deem best."

"Prophet?" Elder Horado cleared his throat.

Rhett didn't want to look at the marsh deer. He knew what was coming.

"Prophet, I'm not sure this would be in keeping with the law."

Anger brewed inside Rhett like water from an underground spring. *How dare he check me on the law!*

"The law is my business, Elder Horado," Rhett retorted in a quick manner.

Everyone went silent. The marsh deer's shoulders slumped along with Rhett's spirit. "I'll consider your proposition, Elder Cletus. Thank you."

Rhett closed the Council and disappeared into the upper branches of the Wimba without a word to anyone. He felt both remorse at how he had spoken to Elder Horado and excitement at the possibility of getting Fattima out of his fur. "Yes, the idea has merit and lots of it," he assured himself loud enough for even the youngest of Wimba birds still wet in the nest to hear.

Discussion Questions

1. Why does Rhett become angry when Elder Horado questions him about the law? How should have Rhett responded?

2. Rhett keeps trying to solve the problems on his own. How is that working out for him? What should he be doing instead?

Chapter

27

Monkey Justice

"**R**hett, come quick!" Mara's voice penetrated the heavy smoke of Rhett's now ever-recurring nightmare.

"Rhett, are you there?" She hollered from the base.

"Coming." He tried to yell with a scratchy voice before clearing the sleep phlegm from his throat. He took a second to stretch his limbs and tail. Both were tense from his nightmare, but at least Mara had pulled him away before the searing pain had started.

Scampering down slower than usual, he landed on the dirt at the base with a thud. "What's up?"

"Rhett, you gotta come see this - quick. It's terrible!"

His fur pricked like a porcupine with the words, and he looked up into the Wimba branches. "Where are the messengers? Why didn't they wake me if something was wrong?"

"They're too busy tittering to every creature that will open an ear about your plan to give Fattima a portion of Sanchia."

Rhett jerked his head back to stare at Mara. "What! I was considering. It wasn't definite."

153

Mara raised an eyebrow. "We need to talk later, but first, you gotta see this." With that, she shot off across the Sanctuary leaving Rhett no choice but to follow in her dust trail.

The two kinkajous made quick time to the northern border where an old mango grove stood at the base of the cliffs. Brittle shards crunched in Rhett's paws as he took hold of the sprawling branches, a contrast from the normal glossy green mango leaves. Mara dropped down to the ground near the end of the grove and faced the cliffs. *Why is she stopping here? She can't climb the cliffs.*

Rhett dropped beside her, put his paws on his knees, and panted hard from the fast fly. Mara faced the tree to her left, one whose branches butted against the cliff face. Hanging upside down with his legs held fast by a rope of vines was a young capuchin. His eyes bulged, but he wasn't seeing anything—not anymore. Blood ran in small crimson streams down his white fur, shading him the color of a blushed orchid. His belly was bloated—its covering layer of skin stretched taut. At least one arm twisted and dangled underneath his body at an unnatural angle, and there were numerous, blue-tinted welts adorning his head.

The ghastly image held Rhett prisoner until Mara's words set him free. "They say it was an accident, the monkeys that is. But, Rhett, this was no accident. Look," and she paused pointing at the ground underneath the capuchin. "There are the sticks they used."

Sure enough, three sticks, twice the thickness of his tail, peeked out of the thick grass at the base of the mango tree.

"Why?" he said, voice cracking at the end. "Why would they do that to one of their own?"

"My guess is he stole someone's food. That seems to be the common vice of late." She looked to him, knowing her words would remind him of Dex.

"Why didn't they bring him to Council? There are laws against food theft, laws that would have provided justice and well, protection for…"

154

"Protection, Rhett? Like Dex? He's never going to pay those mangoes back. His time's running out, and he'll be banished. Maybe this monkey's death was at least quick."

Rhett hung his head in shame. He regretted the strict punishment he had given Dex. It was the punishment given during normal times—hard but not harsh. He had been trying to think of a way around his order without losing face. He pushed aside the thought. He'd have to figure that out—but not now—not while a dead capuchin hung in front of him.

"It could have been settled better than this." He whispered.

Mara shrugged but then didn't say anything else about Dex. After a moment, she nodded toward the capuchin. "Well, what are you going to do?"

Rhett hated that question. The responsibility weighing on him felt heavier than a beached dolphin. He pawed at the grass, relieved that at least some remained in Sanchia. "I guess I need to talk to Mateo."

He peeked at Mara out of the corner of his eye. She stared at him, waiting for more. "It's just … I told him to go his own way last time we talked. What am I supposed to tell him now?"

"But this is too much, Rhett. There are limits to how far the creatures can go their own way. This is wrong."

Hanging his head, Rhett knew she was right. Sanchia couldn't survive like this, not for any length of time.

Mara continued. "And Rhett, the same goes with your plan to let Fattima have her way with the northern region. You can't just let the creatures rule themselves. This kinda stuff will happen more and more. Before you know it, we'll all be living in chaos."

Rhett felt the gravity of her words. What kinda Prophet was he? Certainly not anything like Saloma. Ultimately, he was responsible for this monkey's death. If he had kept control of the primates, this wouldn't have happened. He turned away from Mara, not wanting to meet her eyes, ever again. She would know what an abject failure he was.

He inched away, towards the neighboring tree. "I need to go," he said barely loud enough for her to hear.

"Rhett, you need to talk with Elder Mateo. You can still bring them back into order under the Sovereign and his laws. It's not too late."

"I gotta go, Mara." And with that, he turned and fled to the nearest tree. He swung away with a chant running through his head, "Failure – Failure – Failure."

Discussion Questions

1. What is the difference between failing at something and being a failure?

2. Do you think God ever believes one of His children is a failure? Who are you in God's eyes?

Chapter

28

Wages of Sin

"Finally, the fat monkey isss here." Fattima hissed and proceeded to push out into the middle of the placid creek. She had taken pains in the afternoon to set the scene just so, and now she floated ready, head resting above water on a fallen branch saved for such an occasion. The moon steadily rose over the canopy line, its rays reflecting in diamonds across the face of the muddy water. The sparkles excited her, and what excited her, enhanced her hunger.

Fattima listened as Mateo crashed through the nearby underbrush. She had made it abundantly obvious to all that she was cruising this particular creek, hoping he would take the bait. She knew he wanted to speak with her, had heard the squawks of discontent from the hundreds of parrots intent on sharing jungle gossip. The preened princesses of the air loved to flock and share the latest morsel of news. Whereas fowl were usually a source of annoyance for Fattima, on occasion, they proved useful.

The beefy spider monkey burst through the brush onto the narrow beachhead. Mateo stopped and studied the waters, squinting through narrow cracks that Fattima knew could no longer see clearly.

"Ssssupurb evening, isssn't it, Elder?" hissed Fattima.

Mateo relaxed and dropped down to all fours, straining to catch his breath with large huffs. The arduous trek along the creek had sapped him of his wind.

"Fattima, I heard you might be here. I need to speak with you."

"Yesssss, Elder. Alwayssss at your ssservice."

Elder Mateo sat up at the tone of politeness and rested his forearms on his massive knees. His white belly protruded from his legs and sparkled along with the water in the moonlight. Fattima could hardly suppress her writhing. She tensed her belly muscles, keeping them in check in case her anticipation unwittingly caused a small tidal wave.

"Fattima," Mateo started. "This whole business of ruling ourselves is not working out like you promised. I got monkeys raiding outside our territory, monkeys stealing, monkeys killing. Once I told them they didn't have to listen to Rhett anymore, they took that to mean they didn't have to pay attention to no one, including me."

"Elder." Fattima implored. "Come a little closser, won't ya? You know these sssorry slitsss of mine can't hear half as well as your earsss. Hmmm were you sssaying sssomething about raiding?"

Mateo huffed in annoyance but used his massive arms to help push him to the water's edge. The water gently lapped over the furry sticks called legs now jabbing into the water like sharp branches.

"Yes, Fattima. Raiding and stealing and killing. There's no controlling the young ones anymore. They practically murdered one of our own yesterday, and I'm not even sure who all was involved. And I'm still getting all sorts of flak about Brutus and Bruno from the older monkeys. You remember the brothers, Brutus and Bruno. They died, or at least as good as died, on that boat mission of Rhett's."

Fattima turned one ear toward the emerging moon. "What, Elder? Did you sssay the brothers ssspied on Rhett? Good job, Elder. That wassss a brilliant plan."

"No, Fattima!" Mateo shook his massive head and stepped closer to Fattima floating three tail lengths away. "It wasn't a brilliant plan.

The brothers died taking your advice to not listen to Rhett. I know they took it too far, didn't think it through, but I can't be there for every decision. How are my monkeys supposed to think for themselves? They've been taught all their lives to listen to orders, and then we go and tell them to disobey Rhett whenever they like. Brut and Brun didn't know the difference between an order and common sense. If they'd have, they'd still be here."

"Oh." Fattima answered, "that's a ssshame." And she looked down into the water for a moment of silence, prompting the spider monkey to do the same.

"I'm not done, Fattima. For the record, I was not on board with Tomás dying. You never mentioned killing him. We have no quarrel with the marsh deer. The whole thing was a bit extreme in my opinion."

Fattima didn't answer, just stared into the water as if again mourning the mention of the dead. The old monkey didn't go along with the mourning ritual this time but got up and paced the edge of the creek, sending shards of water in all directions as he stomped through the mud.

"Fattima!" Mateo called, stepping a bit closer, white belly now floating like a ripe mango on the water's surface. "Fattima, are you listening?"

"Oh, yesssss, Elder. I hear perfectly."

Mateo cocked his head. "Then what do you have to say? The other regions you talked about, how do they get along with no Prophet, no law?"

Fattima's branch floated closer to the spider monkey, now only a tail length away. "Maybe their monkeysss posessss sssomeseennssssse?"

It took a breath for Elder Mateo to catch her meaning, but when understanding dawned, he angrily slapped his forearm onto the surface of the creek. No one dared talk to Mateo like that. Water spewed in all directions, and Mateo inevitably closed his eyes against the onslaught of water droplets. When he opened his eyes, now

159

blurry, Fattima was nowhere in sight. "Fattima?" he hollered twisting from side to side, his perilous position becoming apparent even to him.

"I'm here, Mateo." Fattima answered from behind. "Sssa,sssa,sssa," she laughed. "You, my ssstupid monkey, are no longer needed."

Mateo's eyes widened like the mouth of the Great River. He thrashed arms and legs and even head in his attempt to return to shore. He called for help, but the jungle paid no mind.

"Fattima, you better not. I'll …"His words ended abruptly as he realized the futility and tried once more to surge for land.

Strong vines seized his legs, his belly, his shoulders. Mateo lost his balance and plunged face first into the shallows. A splash like the fall of a great Kapok came and went unheeded by any nearby creatures. The spider monkey's paws dug trenches in the soft mud as he fought against the serpent's pull—dragging him deeper under the water. He managed to take in a gulp of air and begin what would have been a jungle-shaking scream but ended up being only a strange gurgling sound. Mateo's head sank out of sight; his orange tuff of hair swaying under the surface, waving the world goodbye.

Bubbles floated up for several minutes as if revealing a secret opening to an underground hot spring. But then stillness reigned again, and the branch that Fattima had rested upon floated lazily down creek.

Discussion Questions

1. Do you feel like Mateo got what he deserved? Why or why not?

2. What do we deserve for our sins? Who rescues us from our punishment of eternal death by His grace? Romans 6:23 (NIV) says, "For the wages of sin is death, but the gift of God is eternal life in Christ Jesus our Lord."

Chapter

29

Repentance

*H*ome! *I just want to go home.* Rhett turned—but not to the Wimba—to the braided strangler vine and the sanctuary his mom provided. As he dove into the hollow weave of the strangler vine, he paused to listen for Brianna or his siblings. Not home, as far as he could tell.

At this time of night, they would be out gathering, which meant vainly searching for forgotten fruit while inevitably munching on termites. Always termites for the kinkajous though the thought of eating another one made his insides want to crawl out. But given enough time, his stomach would rumble, and the only solution came in the form of a brown, crunchy insect.

Rhett scaled the strangler vine as quickly as ever but hesitated before poking his head out onto the deck. Brianna could be taking an early evening nap, and he didn't want to get into one of her "discussions." He scanned the area. When satisfied that all was clear, he pawed lightly over to his old nook.

He climbed into the burrowed hole, which was smaller than he remembered as a cub. He sniffed and instantly detected the odor of his siblings, but the scent carried more than that. The woodsy smell was one of safety, plenty, acceptance—the aroma of home.

Settling into a bit of moss, still mused from the twins' recent use, Rhett clucked his tongue. *They get away with messy moss. Mom would have never let me keep such an untidy nook.*

Random thoughts like these floated in and out like dandelion seeds on a breeze. Rhett didn't want to think about Tomás or Fattima or the gruesome scene he'd just witnessed. Weariness followed any attempt to solve the food crisis, and he was oh so weary already. Praying wasn't on his want-to-do list either, but the unbidden cry rose from the deep and escaped his lips without his consent. "I'm not good at this Prophet thing, Sovereign. Why'd you pick me?"

He hadn't prayed in moons – couldn't remember his last real prayer. Guilt flooded his soul like the rising of the Great River, swift and powerful. Maybe he should just be quiet. It'd been so long— embarrassingly long.

Tears trickled down Rhett's face and plopped onto the wooden nook floor. *The Sovereign won't listen to me, not after I've ignored Him.* The thought bothered Rhett, more than any of the other thoughts waiting to plague him. *Have I messed up too bad? Gone so far, He won't want me back?*

He stared at the walls surrounding him, and the memory of his first dream came to mind. The Sovereign was real to him then. Now, the walls were lifeless and cold like Tirgato's old pit. He had to try; his heart ached with desire for it to be right again.

"Sovereign, I'm sorry. I'm sorry I got mad at you for not fixing the food shortage. I'm sorry for not respecting your law, for trying to figure things out on my own. I feel like I've failed you and everybody. I tried to do what seemed like smart things, but I messed everything up. Please forgive me. Please give me wisdom to wait on your answer, to trust that you are working in your own time. Please help me be the Prophet you want me to be."

Rhett didn't hear an audible answer. No writing appeared on the nook's wooden walls. But after his prayer, he felt peace blow into his heart like a cool breeze across the canopy top. He hadn't felt that in a long time. Not only was he forgiven, but his path didn't seem as daunting anymore. He didn't have to figure everything out on his own; he just had to listen to the Sovereign and speak when He said speak and swing when He said swing.

Moonlight shadows crept across the floor of the platform; gusts of wind blew dust tornados up into the canopy. But inside his nook—calmness. A peace blanketed him like a cover of dry leaves in the rainy season. He could rest now: rest from guilt, from worry, from waiting decisions. The Sovereign was in control.

Discussion Questions

1. Why might it be difficult to start praying again after you've fallen out of the habit?

2. Have you ever experienced the peace of God amid a storm?

Chapter

30

A Dream Come True

"**C**rack!" The electrifying bolt jarred Rhett out of his dream.

"What's that?" he murmured in a high-pitched voice, his fur already on edge. He looked out of his nook and saw his mom huddled beside the opposite support tree. She stared at him, fear rounding her brown eyes.

"It's storming something fierce, Rhett. Storming, but no rain. Not one drop."

Rhett climbed out of his old nook and scampered across the platform toward Brianna. The wind blew a massive gust, and his claws gripped the platform to keep steady. "Where are the twins?"

"I told them to get in my nook when I saw you in theirs." She glanced into the hole she guarded and gave a half grin. "Teen kinkajous can sleep through anything."

Rhett rubbed his tail. The nightmare had once again struck with a vengeance. This time, so many more details had come into focus.

"Mom, I had the dream again, but more of it this time. I saw the creek and it…"

164

Another crack of thunder interrupted Rhett. So close he felt the shock rattle his bones.

He turned his ear and listened for a moment. "There it is," he whispered in amazement, "the small crackle of leaves." He sniffed. "Yes, the dream has begun."

Rhett turned to Brianna with both authority and urgency in his voice. "Listen carefully. Take the twins now to the Wimba. Stop along the way and get Mara and her mom, but don't tarry. And do not, whatever happens, leave the Sanctuary. Stay at the base of the Wimba."

The twins whimpered and poked their heads out. Brianna looked nervously at them and back to Rhett. "What's wrong, Rhett? Where are you going?"

"It's the fire, Mom, from my dream. I need to go now; I need to warn what animals will still listen. The Sanctuary will be safe, one of the few areas in Sanchia. Now hurry and go. Stay there!"

Rhett turned toward the strangler vine door.

"Wait!" Brianna called, stopping him. She scampered over to him and placed her paw on his shoulder. "Sovereign, please give Rhett wisdom, help him lead. Please keep him and all your creatures safe under your care."

Her eyes opened and connected with his before she squeezed his shoulder and nudged him out the door.

✳✳✳

"Where are the beavers?" he asked the surrounding air, heavy-laden with smoke. The flames had overtaken the eastern border faster than a flash flood in rainy season. Embers bombarding his tail, he had traveled north along the bank of the Flujo de Vida on Sanchia's eastern border, warning as many animals as he could find. He had also sent as many birds as he could wrangle into service to spread the news along the western border.

To make matters worse, he had received news that the birds of prey had gathered just outside the western quadrant. All those who dared seek shelter in the barren wastelands would become effortless targets for the harpy eagles, the falcons, the vultures, and the hawks. The fowl had sensed the fire almost as soon as he had and had flocked to the west in anticipation of an easy feast.

The south was hemmed in by the Great River and the initial spread of fire along the eastern banks. The north was closed by the cliffs to all except the monkeys. It was here by the old mango grove that he sat waiting where the Flujo de Vida flowed down from the steep northern cliffs. The rushing water, the second largest in Sanchia after the Great River would travel along the eastern border, dividing Sanchia from Fortez and emptying out in the Great River not far from where the fire began.

If only he could urge the beavers to hurry. They still had time to build the dam he had seen in his dream. The dam would reroute the water to flow through the center of Sanchia by way of Pooto Creek. The resulting floodwaters would hopefully be enough to stop the northwestern expansion of the fire and save many Sanchians. That is if the Sanchians chose to listen to his advice and seek refuge in the Sanctuary. The Sovereign had revealed the plan to him in his dream. Now that he was living his dream, it was clearer than ever. If the animals strayed to the south or the east of the Wimba, fire would await them. The north was blocked, and if they went west, the birds of prey gathered on the badlands—waiting.

Even during his frantic swing here, he could tell many of the creatures would pay no heed to his cries of warning. Some would listen, yes, and go right away to the Sanctuary, but most would run in circles and perish. They yelled to him as he passed, "Why would we go there? It's foolishness."

Rhett tried to explain as much as he could without spending too much time in any one place. "The Sovereign told me; all creatures will find safety in the Sanctuary." Some scoffed at his words, some ignored, but some would listen and be saved.

Relief came when Elder Cletus poked his head out of the brown marsh grass and waddled to shore. "Fire coming, Prophet."

Rhett resisted the urge to roll his eyes. "Yes, Elder. I know. I need your help."

The old beaver hawed and patted his tail nervously on the sand. "Well, Prophet. I didn't even want to waste time coming here, but that blue bird of yours kept chattering on. I'm planning to swim our families north away from this fire. Why would we be sticking around in hot water with flames lapping our whiskers?"

"Send your families to the Wimba, Cletus. They'll be safe there. I need you and your best builders to put up a dam—a strong one—and quick."

"A dam?" the elder spit out. "Why are you talking about dams? There's a fire to worry about."

Rhett breathed hard and looked over his shoulder. He didn't have time for this. He still needed to warn the rest of the northern quadrant not to panic and attempt to find refuge in the badlands. "Look, Cletus. Build a dam across this stretch of beach. Build it at least two tails above the current water line. Make sure the dam can hold. It'll reroute the water to Pootocreek and flow along the western side of the Sanctuary. The mass flow of water should be enough to stop the spread of the fire. Do you understand?"

The old beaver's tail had stopped slapping the shoreline mud. He stared at Rhett as if he had never seen a kinkajou before. "How'd you figure that out?"

"I didn't. The Sovereign did. Now are you going to help?" Rhett danced from one leg to the other. He needed to swing.

Cletus nodded. "You can count on us beavers, Prophet. We'll get it done." And with a quick dive, he disappeared into the muddy creek.

Discussion Questions

1. Is it easier to obey when you know all the reasons behind the order?

2. Why is it important to follow God and those in authority who we trust even when we don't understand the reasons?

3. In what situations do we NOT obey others?

Chapter

31

Salvation in the Sanctuary

R hett sounded warning calls along the northern border until his voice croaked like a crusty cane toad. "Go to the Wimba. Seek shelter in the Sanctuary. Go now. The fire is heading this way."

When he reached the northwest border where the cliffs dropped sharply into the badlands, he paused for breath and surveyed the open landscape. Eagles, hawks, falcons, and vultures had temporarily forgotten any interspecies squabbles. They flew as one dark mass that looked very much like the heavy smoke clouds that rose to meet them from the east. Rhett thought about all the animals he had warned to go to the Wimba and not to try their luck in the badlands. Too many didn't listen. He could see from his perch on an outlying mango tree, the occasional, purposeful dive of a hawk.

Right before Rhett turned away from the ghastly view, he spotted a dust cloud mushrooming from the north. It looked like a herd of peccaries rooting bugs in a sand pit. He wasn't expecting travelers from the north, especially from the wastelands. He lifted his nose to investigate, but a breeze came up on his back, and the attempt only left him coughing up smoke.

He'd have to figure that mystery out later. Turning back toward the Sanctuary, his heart ached for the animals who had failed to listen to his warning, but what more could he do? It was time to see if the beavers had done their job. Swinging south along the empty corridor of Calabash Creek, Rhett prayed, "Please let the creek swell wide enough to protect Sanchia's faithful ones." As he swung closer to the Wimba, the smoke, filling the top branches of the canopy, became so thick that Rhett had to drop and cruise under the gray blanket.

Swinging low along Calabash Creek was normally avoided for two reasons: its dense foliage and its abundance of moonflowers which reek with the scent of monkey armpit. The night bats love the smell and gleefully screech the evenings away along the creek. There was a stark absence of both the pungent smell of the moonflower and the high-pitched cries of the bats. He missed both, and this had to be the first time in his life that he missed either. But the familiar memories circled around in his brain, distracting him from worry as he traveled from one vine to the next, sounding warning calls in cadence with his swing.

Rhett heard the mass of Sanchians several palm tree lengths before he landed on the outskirts of the Sanctuary. Animals were packed flesh to flesh into every square inch of open field. Lizards and frogs of countless colors crawled in and out between the paws and hooves of agoutis, anteaters, marsh deer, squirrels, capuchins, peccaries, and spider monkeys. *They came, well some of them came,* and he breathed a sigh of relief. *But how am I going to get to the Wimba from here?*

He pushed his way into the crowd but made little progress. Azul, who always hovered near, squawked, "Make room, make room for Prophet, make room!" An astute marsh deer bent his head to block Rhett's intended path. "There's a quicker way, Prophet, climb on."

Perched between two velvet-trimmed antlers, Rhett had a bird's eye view of the Sanctuary. The oval-topped heads of the crowded creatures dotted the field like lily pads in a pond. He hopped from the deer's head onto the top of a neighbor and so on in his path toward the Wimba. A few protested the intrusion until kinkajou pass became a game for the creatures, a distraction from the looming smoke above.

Soon, the Prophet landed non-too-smoothly at the base of the Wimba. His mom watched and waited for him, wringing her paws. "I told her to stay, Rhett. I begged her to, but she wouldn't."

Rhett's relief to be back safely at the Wimba disappeared faster than a fly at a frog festival. "Who?" Rhett asked, "Who are you talking about?" But he already knew; the answer was written all over his mom's face. Beside Brianna sat Mara's mom staring blank eyed at the approaching smoke cloud.

"Why did she leave? I told you to stay put." Rhett twisted around, frantically searching the sea of animals, hoping to see her face pop up in sight.

"It's my fault." Brianna covered her eyes. "I forgot about the Yano cubs sleeping in the Kapok nook. They're new orphans, remember, the ones who didn't make it out on the last re-homing trip."

Rhett shook her shoulder with his paw. "Mom, which Kapok? Where exactly did she go?"

"The Trinal."

"The Trinal! That's spitting distance from the initial fire line."

Brianna nodded without raising her eyes. "I tried to stop her, Rhett. I should have gone instead. But the twins? I stopped to think about the twins, and then before I knew it, she had left."

Rhett looked over at Mara's mom. She sat tall like a tree, hadn't moved, even an eye twitch. "I'll get her. Don't worry." Paying no attention to his mom's pleas to reconsider, he leapt up to the platform and stared out over the crowd. He'd have to make his way now to the far eastern section of the Sanctuary. From his vantage point, he could see the rerouted Pooto creek flowing freely. At least that part of the plan had gone well.

Smoke billowed over the strand of water, carrying with it the occasional orange ember. The fire was near, so close that the creek would soon be tested as a firebreak solution. His paws seemed rooted to the Wimba in despair. *No, I won't think that way. I don't know that she's not safe. Maybe she's already made it back.* Without warning, he jumped onto the surprised head of a taller animal within range and skipped atop creature to creature toward the fire.

Discussion Questions

1. Wildfires, hurricanes, earthquakes, floods, and blizzards are all natural disasters that affect wildlife and humans. Why does God allow them to happen? What good may come from them?

2. Mara didn't hesitate to risk her life to save the two orphans. What makes people willing to die for others?

Chapter

32

Jungle Inferno

Rhett was almost at the creek when he noticed a small group of animals huddled on the far side. *Why don't they swim over? It's not so wide; they'd make it easy.* His question was soon answered when he paused on the head of a howler monkey and looked out onto the flowing waters of the Pooto. Writhing snakes, hundreds of them, swirled just beneath the surface eddies. He growled, startling a few of the animals underneath him. "I can't stand opportunist hunters. They have no conscience."

Perhaps hearing the Prophet's grumble, Fattima emerged—plopping her enormous head on the bank of the Sanctuary. The animals along the creek side recoiled and fell back on one another. "Greetingssss, Prophet. Sssweltering day, isssn't it? Won't you come cool off? Sa-sa-sa."

Rhett met her evil gaze and then jumped the few feet that separated them to land in the shallows. "Kill me if you dare, Fattima. The Sovereign's judgment on you will be swift." The frank warning and sudden splash of the water startled the snake, and she pulled back under the surface without another word.

"Rhett." Mara called from across the water. Eyes burning, the Prophet squinted into the smoke that hung like morning mist over the creek. Mara held two small kinkajous, one tucked under each arm. But they weren't alone. A small family of capuchins gathered close, anxiously looking back and forth from Mara to Rhett. In addition, three squirrels ran circles around the others in nervous hysterics.

A crack split the air, and the top of a towering mahogany crashed into the undergrowth, only a few tail lengths from the creek. Red hot shards showered the crowd on both sides of the bank. The little huddled band opposite Rhett screamed and dropped to their knees, arms folding over their ears to protect against the onslaught of fiery sparks. All except the squirrels, who increased their frantic lapping and inserted a lap between the legs of the capuchins.

Think fast, Rhett! What to do? What to do? The Prophet paced along the bank, hoping the answer would rain down like the orange embers now pelting the Sanctuary grass. The animals nearest him had backed up, either avoiding a lurking Fattima or the Mahogany embers.

"Got it." He screamed to no one in particular. "Azul." He looked behind where he knew the bright blue bird would be hovering. "I'm going over there. Look for me in that tree directly behind the group." He pointed to a medium-sized Brazil Nut tree with woody liana vines hanging off it like the hairy legs of a tarantula. "When you see me, come fetch one of the ends of the vine and carry it back over here." Rhett looked up and saw that Elder Horado had squeezed his way through the crowd and stood ready to assist. "Give the end to Horado. Elder, bite and hold onto that vine with all your might."

The deer noddedbut then asked, "How you getting over there?" With his question, he looked at the creek, half expecting Fattima and her friends to fly out of the water at them.

"I need a sloth."

Horado just cocked his head and stared, but Azul lifted off the ground and gave the call to the other birds to find the nearest sloth. Of course, all the sloths were huddled near the edge of the Sanctuary, not willing to expend one twig of energy more than necessary. Rhett knew their power, though, had seen it from Saloma on occasions when she was willing to play or show off a bit.

"Azul!" Rhett hollered in his wake. "Choose big … and male."

The marsh deer stared at him like he would a teen capuchin who had consumed an unhealthy number of rotten mangos. Rhett sighed—he didn't have time to explain. "Elder Horado, please follow Azul and fetch the nearest sloth. If I have to wait for the sloth to crawl here, it'll be too late."

The marsh deer, understanding at least this directive, followed Azul's lead to the nearest sloth. With the aid of the bird's insistent bossing, Horado prodded the reluctant creature to climb on his neck.

Horado delivered Ivan, the sloth, to Rhett in record time despite the crowded conditions. When Ivan landed on the creek bank, he looked down at Rhett, terror in his eyes. Pity, and a bit of nostalgia, pinged the Prophet's heart. He looked like a younger version of Saloma, gray hair just starting to peek out in patches along his back. His arms hung long, with sinewy muscles rippling down from massive shoulders.

"Ivan, it's okay. But I need you to do something for me, something that will take a lot of energy but will hopefully save those creatures' lives." Rhett nodded toward the huddled group on the opposite shore.

"What cccan I do, Prophet?"

"I need you to throw me across."

Ivan's mouth dropped open. "Ppprophet, I can't throw you. I can't throw anything."

Rhett put on his best impression of Saloma 'instructing' him in school. "Ivan, you can throw me. I saw Saloma one time throw rocks twice my size."

Ivan shook his head and looked at the ground.

"You can do it, Ivan. I know you can. And we must hurry."

"What if I mmmiss, Prophet? What if I don't throw you far enough?"

"Well, then, I'll get wet, won't I!" Rhett answered with a cheeky grin, choosing not to point out the snakes to Ivan. "Now, hurry up. Get up your strength and throw me like you would an annoying squirrel who just woke you up from a nap."

Ivan grinned—just slightly and from only one side of his mouth. But it was enough, Rhett knew he had tickled the truth. A second later, he was in the air—flying like Azul. He landed on the other side with a thud in the mud, just shy of dry land. He quickly gave Ivan a wave of thanks. Without even addressing an astonished Mara, he darted up the nearby Brazil Nut tree.

The liana vine he needed would have to be not only strong but long enough to stretch across the creek. The one he initially wanted was fastened in too many places. It would take precious minutes to chew all the holds. He leaned down to holler, "Mara, can you help? The monkeys too?"

Rhett tugged at another promising vine. *Yes, this one will work.* He chewed the liana joints along the trunk while Mara and the family of capuchins scampered over, all of which had surmised his plan by now. The set of twins clung tightly to Mara's neck, not wanting to be put down for a second. The squirrels shifted from circling the group to circling the base of the Brazil Nut tree.

A capuchin chewed the last knot near the base, and Azul quickly grabbed the vine in his beak. In only a few flaps, he flew to Horado's side. Vine now secure, Rhett and Mara scampered down to the squirrels. He had to physically shake the shoulders of one to get them to look up at the hairy liana now stretched across Pooto Creek. One glance is all it took though. Wasting no time, the squirrels crossed the vine, followed closely by the monkey family.

Mara looked at Rhett, her brown eyes shiny and wet. *Why is she still here?*

"Hurry, Mara." He said and motioned for her to go. Both young kinkajous, still hanging tight around her neck, buried their heads in her neck scared of crossing an open vine over snake-infested waters.

But Mara was young, quick, and strong. She easily scaled the Brazil Nut with both clinging cubs and Rhett on her tail.

Just as she stepped out onto the vine, the crown from a neighboring palm crashed down on top of the Brazil Nut. Mara screamed. Rhett lunged for her and grabbed her by the waist, pulling all three kinkajous to his chest as the trunk shook violently under the burning weight. Flames burst through the air around them. The heat seared his face and paws like a thousand midday suns. The tree stopped swaying long enough for Rhett to get his bearing and test the vine. "It still holds." He hollered to Mara. "Go now."

She gave him a pleading look, but he yelled, "Go, Mara!" and pushed her toward safety. He could barely see Elder Horado on the other side, still biting down on the vine while straining his neck to spot them. Rhett gripped his side of the vine with all four paws, tail looped around the trunk. The vine was tethered somewhere above, or at least it had been before the crash. But how close the vine hold was to the fire now, he could not say. Not wanting to take a chance of it breaking on his end with Mara and the cubs stretched out above the snakes, he pulled the vine close to him.

A stiff breeze chose that instant to blow through and stir up the fire below. Smoke and ash mushroomed up and enveloped the Brazil Nut. Squinting, he tried to follow Mara's path through the swirling orange and gray haze. He opened his mouth to call her name. He had to know if she was safe. But the cracking sound that came out couldn't compete with the overpowering roar of the fire.

She had to be over by now. He tested the vine with a yank, and it held. Time to scurry home.

The thought of Mara and the twins safe on the other side made him smile. *This will all be over soon.* The comforting thought eased the scratchy pain in his throat and the burn on his ear from where a flying ember had nested in his fur.

When he leaped onto the vine bridge, all was well for the blink of a bat's eye until an explosion from above vibrated the Brazil Nut. Then all movement—all time—ceased while Rhett hung in open air.

The vine had given way, and even though the kinkajou still clutched the hairy strand in desperation; gravity could not be stopped. Free-fall wind parted the fur on Rhett's back as he plunged toward the jungle floor.

He screamed right before his tail found and gripped a jagged branch; the sudden jerk swinging and spreading his legs and arms like a thrown-out banana peel. Relief was pursued by a sense of panic. He couldn't stay here, he had to swing to a safer perch.

Rhett looked up, but he could only see black with red streaks of lightning – down was no better. *How close am I to the ground? Can I drop and try to make the edge of the creek?* But then there were the snakes. In their frenzied state, would they even recognize his Prophet marking?

Searing pain shot up his tail, alerting every muscle. He must swing away—but where? "Where are the branches?" he screamed again in confusion while craning his head in all directions. The trees still standing were stripped of branches, bark, foliage of any kind. They looked like black snakes hanging limp from a golden sky.

"Jump!" He yelled, prodding himself to leap into the unknown in hopes of finding a safer branch somewhere lower. But his body wouldn't respond. A searing pain shot up his tail. The branch he clung to shimmered with flashing orange streaks. His tail released, and the Prophet disappeared into a cloud of gray ash.

His last thought before dropping into the burning underbrush was ...*My dream. I remember. This was in my dream.* And then, all went black.

Discussion Questions

1. Rhett knew Ivan the sloth's abilities better than Ivan knew them himself. When others tell us we can do something that might look scary or difficult, how apt are we to believe them? Whom should we trust to lead us to stretch and try new things?

2. John 15:13 says, "Greater love has no one than this: to lay down one's life for one's friends." (NIV) Rhett sacrifices for Mara and

the others in a true act of selfless love. Who would you be willing to sacrifice for? Who do you know would sacrifice for you?

Chapter

33

Snake Supper

Giran smelled the smoke in the badlands from creek lengths away. Fear rose like undigested pork in his throat. He pushed his tribe hard, even harder when he saw the gathered birds of prey. By the time the tribe had reached the Sanctuary, it was packed snout to snout. Even though he had warned his tribe about hunting in the Sanctuary, their eyes flashed with desire—their fangs dripped with drool. It had been a long trip through the wasteland. The cats would resist on his word, but it would take effort.

The animals saw the jaguars with their roaming, hungry eyes and backed away enough for them to approach the Wimba. Brianna perched on the platform where Rhett should have been. The small kinkajou, with her twins huddled around her tail, stared in the opposite direction, not paying heed even to the approaching clan of cats.

"Brianna, where's Rhett? Giran hollered over the deafening din of stressed animals and fire. She turned and stared down at him with a haunted wide-eyed look. *Does she even recognize me?*

Something must have registered because she gave a sudden cry of "Giran" and practically dove headfirst down the Wimba. On the

180

ground beside him, she clung to his arm, shaking him while alternately looking at him and then into the distance. "Giran, you got to help him. He went to find Mara, and I'm afraid both are trapped in the fire."

Pointing in the direction of the incoming fire line with one paw, she shielded her face with the other as if that would help her see through the mass of surrounding creatures. Giran's gaze followed the direction of her quivering outstretched arm. She pointed toward the blackest cloud of smoke. *Surely, Rhett's not in there. He's probably just checking on everyone—will be back any second.* He glanced down at panicked Brianna's face, and that possibility dimmed. "Don't worry, Brianna. I'm going to go find him. Ok?" There was no acknowledgment. Her eyes didn't stray from the direction her arm still pointed.

Giran tried to nose his way through the crowd but didn't get far. "I can't see a thing over all these hides, much less get through." In a surge of frustration, he took a deep breath and roared louder than the rolling of a flash flood, louder even than the sound of the approaching fire. The Wimba vibrated. The creatures stilled with a new terror.

An awed parting of animals allowed Giran to lead his tribe, and Rhett's worried mama, through the throng. The tunnel of creatures opened at the bank of a swollen Pooto Creek. Mara paced the water's edge, eyes locked on the opposite side. Every few seconds, she cried Rhett's name.

"Mara, what happened." Giran yelled, trotting over to her side. "Where's Rhett?"

At the sound of Giran's voice, the kinkajou turned toward the jaguar and practically tackled him. She grabbed at the folds of skin around his neck and pulled him in the direction of the creek, pointing and talking nonsense.

"Mara, stop! Calm down. Tell me where Rhett is."

Tears flowed, etching curves down her soot-stained face. She trembled so much, Giran worried she might collapse into a brown heap at his feet.

"Giran, he's there," she cried as she pointed at the base of a flaming tree on the other side of the creek.

Giran shook his head. Fire consumed the bank across the creek. He looked down at her in disbelief.

"He just fell in. Right before you came."

Giran stepped into the creek but stopped at her next words. "Giran, there's snakes: anacondas, water cobras, even vipers, everywhere."

The jaguar looked back at her and then into the faces of his tribe who had faithfully followed him through the crowd. Elder Ramiro, Cora, her sisters, and the cousins he had grown to respect and love all nodded their silent understanding. They knew what to do. He could almost hear the relieved growling of stomachs.

Giran stayed put while Ramiro and the others stepped forward, around him, and into the water. Leading the triangular shaped attack formation, Ramiro rushed the creek with Giran in the back center. Giran wouldn't engage, not in this fight; he was on the hunt for a kinkajou.

The brown water turned white with swirling foam as teeth and claw connected with prey. The writhing bodies of half-dead snakes landed on shore one by one, tossed high in the air by the ferocious cats. Teams of jaguars dragged the larger serpents to land, with one immobilizing the head, the other bearing the weight.

Giran took little notice of the carnage around him. He would feast later. He swam hard, soon leaving Ramiro and his clan behind. As he neared the shore, he squinted, searching through the smoke for his friend.

He emerged on the other side of the creek dripping wet but knew better than to shake. Soaked with creek water, he plunged into the underbrush where Rhett had last been seen.

It didn't take long for the water to burn away. Giran tensed under the sting of what felt like a thousand electric eels. He couldn't smell past the acrid odor lodged in his nostrils; he couldn't see past his whiskers. "Sovereign, help me. Please help me find Rhett."

The heat of the fire was becoming too intense. He couldn't breathe; he had to turn back. A few more feet: he could make it a few more feet. Then his paw stumbled on something out of place, something small and furry.

"Rhett?" he cried, but the lump on the ground gave no answer. He nudged it with his nose, and yes, even with all the smoke, he could still detect a small hint of kinkajou scent. He found what he thought was his neck and picked him up with his teeth.

Never had Giran felt or dreamt anything so refreshing as when he submerged his burning hide into the depths of Pooto Creek. The area was quickly becoming vermin free. What snakes his kinsman weren't feeding on, had quickly headed north or south away from the hunting party. He made sure to dip Rhett into the blissful coolness a few times as well, hoping the water would help. Mara and Briana had walked out a ways into the creek to usher Rhett and Giran into the Sanctuary.

On shore—a hair from the water's edge—the girls dug a shallow hole and indicated for Giran to place Rhett into the cavity. Then they covered the Prophet in cool creek mud, all except his head and tail. His head was kept out for breathing. There wasn't much left of his tail, just a black nob attached to his hind end.

Brianna put her cheek next to Rhett's mouth. Knowing what she was about, the watching animals collectively held their breath. Even the jaguars stopped their feast and silently awaited the verdict.

Her ears perked straight. "He's breathing." She announced in a loud yet broken voice. Mara exhaled and collapsed in a relieved heap by Rhett's mud pile.

Giran, wanting to believe Brianna but not quite sure, stooped down to lick Rhett's face. Brianna cocked her head in question. Between licks, he explained. "Licking works wonders for cats, no reason it can't work for kinkajous too." Brianna just shrugged and turned her attention back to Rhett.

"Enough with the tongue," came a weak voice.

The barely audible comment from the Prophet elicited cheers and cries of joy from the crowd. "The Prophet is alive!" rose an echoing chant across the Sanctuary field.

Rhett opened his eyes and smiled up at Giran, creating dirt cracks in his cheeks. Giran knew his friend would have greeted him differently had he been able—a greeting that probably would have involved him swinging laps around his neck. As it was, Rhett was stuck in the mud and would be for quite some time while his skin healed.

The jaguars, realizing the immediate crisis was over, resumed their snake supper. Typically, one would frown upon a predator feast on Sanctuary ground, but considering the circumstances, no one spouted the finer points of the law.

Giran walked over to Cora and her sisters. They had managed to drag up the absolute largest anaconda Giran had ever laid eyes upon. On top of her unusual length, her belly was swollen like she had eaten a tree load of coconuts, perhaps the whole tree itself. She looked vaguely familiar, but he couldn't recall her name. Good thing she no longer swam Sanchian waters.

Discussion Questions

1. Was Giran arriving just in the nick of time coincidence? What would have happened if he had ignored Prophet Sam and delayed his trip even a little?

2. Even though it was against the law to hunt in the Sanctuary, why did no one object to the snake feast?

Chapter

34

Heaven's Precious Jewels

"**W**hy my tail, Giran?" Rhett whined while licking the honey from his arm. "I had such a handsome tail. Mara loved my tail."

Giran hid his smirk by turning away his face. He tried to nod in sympathy. Over the last few days, his friend had graduated from being covered in mud to being plastered with honey. When some of the swarming flies strayed to Giran's side of the Wimba platform, he easily swished them away with his tail. This action produced a longing in the vain kinkajou's eyes. Giran couldn't help but take the opportunity to tease a bit.

"Why don't we find you another one? You know, like a replacement? I can get you one just your size, maybe from a monkey if you didn't want a fellow kinkajou's tail."

The pitiful look on his friend's face turned to a scowl. Giran chuckled. Rhett gave him a stern look that ended up more like a lopsided grin.

"So," broaching a new subject, "when are you going to ask Mara?"

"Ask her what?" Rhett answered with an innocent look, feigning ignorance.

Giran didn't fall for it and cocked his head.

"Well, truth be known." Rhett started and cut an eye at Giran before smoothing out a few more globs of honey on his arm.

"Truth about what?" Giran fished.

"A messenger bird flew north just yesterday to request a "visit" from Blanco's Prophet." A smile spread across the kinkajou's face. "I may have also sent along some herbs and honey so he would bring a couple of mangoes when he returned."

Giran laughed. "That must have cost you quite the stash of herbs."

Rhett joined in the laugh. "All I could beg, barter, and borrow. I actually needed them for a couple of reasons. I, ... I have a little kinkajou friend who's in desperate need of some mangoes." Rhett paused as if taking a lone detour off the path of conversation. There was a story here, but Giran wouldn't push for it right now.

After a moment, Rhett continued. "Annnnnddd, you can't really have a ceremony without at least a few mangoes—drought or no drought. It just can't be."

"So, Blanco's Prophet is coming to perform your covenant ceremony?"

"Yeah, I have no desire to do my ceremony—I'm nervous enough about just being in the ceremony. But I'm not about to let you get the upper paw on me." Rhett smirked. You and Cora's covenant is all anyone in Sanchia talks about. Cora has been whispering to Mara for days all about your ceremony. Cora cries—Mara listens over and over again all dreamy-eyed."

Giran laughed. "That sounds 'bout right."

"I like her by the way." Rhett said. "Cora, I mean."

Giran's face lit up. "What's not to like?"

Whipping between the two friends, a stiff breeze caused both to turn up their noses. There had been the smell of rain earlier, and all the animals stirred in a frenzy of hopeful anticipation. Clouds hovered, but there had been clouds in and out since the passing of the fire. None had carried rain, only the occasional falling of more ash.

"How's the tribe settling in?" Rhett asked, breaking the brief silence.

"Going well so far. Many have found the dens from seasons ago before I was born. Some have chosen to settle closer to the cliffs."

Rhett snorted. "Fond of monkeys?"

Giran smiled, "Very much so."

"Well, now that the jaguars are back, other cats will soon join you. Sanchia will at least be balanced again. If we can ever get rain, maybe we'll have a chance of recovery."

Another minute came and went before Giran spoke again. "Cora and I have settled back in the temple."

Rhett's ears perked. "I didn't think you'd want to live there again."

Giran stroked the platform with his front paw and swatted at a few more flies. "I considered a new den, but I kept coming back to the temple. Mainly because of my mother and the memories I have of her there. They've proven stronger than the ones of Tirgato. Cora liked the place too. It reminds her of the connection we share with Raissa."

Rhett nodded but didn't comment.

Giran went on. "It's amazing how the Sovereign works everything out, isn't it? We couldn't have figured all this out if we had had all the minds of the Amazon."

Rhett flashed a cheeky grin. "Well, brilliant minds like mine are hard to find in abundance."

Giran showed his teeth, and Rhett flung up his arms in mock surrender. "Just kidding."

Both laughed until their sides ached. "It's good to be home." Giran whispered just loud enough for Rhett to hear.

When the friends settled down, they turned again to watch the western sky with interest. The individual clouds had merged into dark masses that were steadily rolling into Sanchian territory. Both silently sought the Sovereign that these would be the ones to end the drought.

Not long after, the first drop plopped on the platform between the two friends and then the second and the third. The Prophet and the elder raised their faces to the heavens, their fur collecting the raindrops like precious jewels. As one, the two friends reverently sighed a prayer of thanks to the Creator. "Sovereign, you are always good, and we give you thanks."

Praise be to the Sovereign, who hears and sees and ever provides for His creation.

Discussion Questions

1. When, where, why, and how do we give God praise?

2. Psalm 15:6 says, "Let everything that has breath praise the Lord. Praise the Lord." Spend some time praising God.

Epilogue

Peace

The temple had taken on a fresh look over the last two seasons. The courtyard was no longer strown with weeds but freshly manicured. Multiple sets of four distinct rake lines crisscrossed the yard's dirt surface—testimony to Giran's fastidious scraping. The neat courtyard appearance was reminiscent of Tirgato's time, but the trailing roses framing the den entrance, the soft and inviting reed mats situated under the shaded regions near the wall—these spoke of better days.

Even with the new décor, it was life that made the largest difference. The birds, once intimidated by Tirgato, now flew in and out of thousands of ancient crevices. The opossums nested in the chinks of the surrounding wall and hung by their long tails from the temple rafters. The Harpy eagle must have also been affected by the changes and decided to finally find a mate, not that it hindered her vigilant watch over the happenings of the temple. While nursing a couple of eaglets, she craned her neck over the side of the nest, intent on monitoring her neighbor, Giran, and his Prophet friend.

"She's dead, Rhett. Dead as in eaten, digested, and you know what else."

"But you're not sure, Giran. Not positive it was her."

The jaguar exhaled a long breath. "Who else could it have been? She was big as a manatee – a pregnant manatee."

Rhett rolled his eyes.

189

"Plus, has Fattima been seen since?"

"No, but half the snakes of Sanchia have disappeared since your little feast."

Giran grinned. "Not a snake wasted! It was a tasty meal after that long trek from Altura. You do remember that I was the last to eat / that day? As a matter of fact, my stomach was growling like a pack of hyenas the entire time I was rescuing you."

Rhett huffed in feigned annoyance. Giran's sacrifice had been mentioned multiple times. But he didn't want to hear about that—he wanted a straight answer to his question, and to hear the answer again and again. He wanted his worry to go away.

"So, you really think Fattima's gone?"

"Rhett," Giran's tone and face now serious, "you need to give it up. Yes, I think she's gone. But regardless, you need to move on. Trust the Sovereign; He's done good by you so far."

Rhett hung his head. "Yeah, you're right."

The massive jaguar swished him with his tail. "As usual, you know."

Rhett looked back at his friend. He would offer up a smart-aleck retort, but Giran unfortunately was right. He couldn't, no wouldn't, debate the wisdom of his friend. He relied on it too much. Instead, a change of topic was in order. "So, have you heard from Altura lately?"

Giran ears perked. "A messenger bird arrived from Prophet Sam just yesterday. Things are going well there—he's back to having Council meetings and has actually unified two more clans: the anteaters and the beavers. It seems like every family in Altura had some petty division or other, from color-of-fur prejudices to the sound of one's bark. He's considering working on the monkeys next but going from beavers to monkeys is a bit ambitious in my opinion—like swimming the rapids after paddling a puddle."

Rhett laughed at his friend's image and shook his head in agreement. "Won't be easy; that's for sure."

The conversation stalled for a moment with both friends staring across the moonlit courtyard, both entertaining their own private musings. The peace was brief, interrupted by two boisterous cubs bounding out of the temple den entrance. Adanna and Ramira ran in zig-zags, nipping at each other's heels and tripping over their own front paws. The two twin jaguars, both beautiful like their mama, were named after their Uncle Adan and Grandpa Ramiro.

"Papa, papa. When will Mama be home?" Adanna questioned between pants for air and nips at her sister.

Giran narrowed his eyes in the direction of his offspring. "You know she'll be home after the cub is born. This is about the fifth time you've asked."

"We can go see the cub then, right? Uncle Rhett, you'll take us, won't you? We want to see your cub right away."

Rhett sighed. Their abundance of energy made Rhett feel like Saloma—moss covered and slower than a slug stuck in deep mud.

Without catching Uncle Rhett's sigh Ramira continued, "How long until she can play? Can we teach her all our games?"

While the Prophet shared their anticipation over his soon-to-be cub, he kept silent, not wanting to disappoint them and dim their excitement. He'd have to explain to them that by the time his cub grew old enough to play, they probably wouldn't be interested in nursery games anymore.

Giran answered instead. "How you girls so sure it's going to be a female cub? Aunt Mara could have a male."

Adanna and Ramira looked at each other, obviously surprised by the thought that the new cub could be something less than their ideal playmate. "Naw," Adanna shook her head, prompting a mirrored action from her sister.

Having consoled themselves that their future fun was intact, both bounded over their father's haunches, one after the other, heading toward the creek that ran alongside the back of the temple. Rhett and Giran couldn't resist joining in the cubs' laughter that sang out in the courtyard like playful puffbirds.

The laughter was chased away with a blur of blue feathers as Azul landed between Rhett and Giran. "Prophet, Prophet. Cub is here. New cub is born."

"What?" Rhett screeched in surprise, jumping up to all fours. "Mara said it wouldn't be until closer to daybreak." He turned to stare at Giran with wide, shock-filled eyes. "Cora said I needed to let Mara rest—said I should check on you."

Giran rolled his eyes. "And you didn't think they might have been getting rid of you for a while?"

Rhett showed no signs of hearing—he was already halfway to the gate.

As the frantic kinkajou raced across the courtyard, dirt and dust flying, Giran hollered in his wake, "Rhett, you want me to run you over there? I can get there quicker."

"Yeah right, Rhett yelled back over his shoulder. "I can still outswing you, tail or no tail." He scurried up one of the stone guards and jumped quick as a flip onto the nearest branch.

The Prophet never flew faster. The trees blended one after another into a smooth runway leading straight to Mara. As soon as Rhett landed in the Sanctuary, he spotted Cora lying down in the shade of the Wimba platform, her keen eyes scanning the field. She had already spotted him and was watching his progress with an amused expression.

When he got within a few tail lengths distance, he stopped, suddenly afraid to go closer. "Is Mara ok? The cub? Is the cub here?"

Cora's head motioned for him to look up. He saw his mom sitting on the platform, her legs dangling and her tail circling in a relaxing rhythm. She was staring right at him, grinning wide. *Ok*, he sighed, *that's gotta be a good sign.*

Rhett launched himself up onto the platform and scurried the remaining distance up the trunk till he approached his living nook. Scared to peek in, he stood motionless, heart racing. His paws were rooted to the branch, his arms locked in terror by his side.

A tiny mewing cry shattered his paralysis. Shaking his head in disgust at himself, he bent and peered into the nook.

Mara rested in a padded nest of leaves, grass, and moss. Her eyes—shiny but excited—greeted him. "Rhett, he's here. He's beautiful. And look how much he's moving already." The little gray bundle nestled on Mara's chest was indeed frantically squirming, trying to crawl every which way to escape Mara's hold. "And he came out squealing like a—like a something." At her flustered attempt to tell him everything at once while tripping over words, the tips of her ears turned an adorable pink. Rhett's heart melted in relief.

Mara stroked the new cub's back while continuing her story. "He wouldn't be quiet until I fed him. Look at him now, he's still fighting for more milk, and he just ate."

"He's going to be quite the paw-full." Rhett agreed, wide smile stretching from ear to ear. He reached a tentative paw into the nest and petted the soft gray fur. The cub stilled under his touch. Rhett's heart swelled five times. He shook his head, trying to understand. *How can I love someone I've just met this much?*

His voice was hoarse when he could finally speak. "I thought maybe, well if you like it, we could name him Carlos. You know, after my dad." He dared a quick glance at Mara. "We don't have to, it's just, I thought…"

Mara grinned up at him, calming his fears. "Rhett, I love it. I was actually hoping you'd suggest it. Brianna and even your dad will be proud."

Mara scooted over, gesturing with a small jerk of her head for Rhett to join her. With his two loves settled close and breathing deep, Rhett shut his eyes and tried to express a prayer to the Sovereign. He shook his head though in helplessness. There was no prayer worthy of the overwhelming feeling of gratefulness in his heart. A simple thanks didn't seem enough. He wanted to say more, wanted to be more.

Drifting in on a breeze, the song of the morning caracaras distracted his prayer. Before he could start again, he heard a whisper.

The quiet words began in his heart, floated out, and echoed around the little nook. "Be still, dear Prophet, be still. My peace is yours."

Discussion Questions

1. Describe a time when you felt God's peace.

2. In Psalm 85:8 (NIV), the Psalmist says, "I will listen to what God the Lord says; He promises peace to His people, His faithful servants…" Praise God for His promise of peace.

*"Now may the Lord of peace Himself
give you peace at all times and in every way.
The Lord be with all of you."*

2 Thessalonians 3:16 (NIV)

About
Kharis Publishing:

Kharis Publishing, an imprint of Kharis Media LLC, is a leading Christian and inspirational book publisher based in Aurora, Chicago metropolitan area, Illinois. Kharis' dual mission is to give voice to under-represented writers (including women and first-time authors) and equip orphans in developing countries with literacy tools. That is why, for each book sold, the publisher channels some of the proceeds into providing books and computers for orphanages in developing countries so that these kids may learn to read, dream, and grow. For a limited time, Kharis Publishing is accepting unsolicited queries for nonfiction (Christian, self-help, memoirs, business, health and wellness) from qualified leaders, professionals, pastors, and ministers. Learn more at: https://kharispublishing.com/

www.ingramcontent.com/pod-product-compliance
Lightning Source LLC
Chambersburg PA
CBHW051422090426
42737CB00014B/2787

9 781637 463857